# GLASGOW
# *the* BEST!
## THE ONE TRUE GUIDE

## Peter Irvine
### *and*
### Graeme Kelling

HarperCollins*Publishers*

HarperCollins Publishers
Westerhill Road, Bishopbriggs, Glasgow G64 2QT

www.**fire**and**water**.com

First published 1998
This updated edition 2000

Reprint 10 9 8 7 6 5 4 3 2 1 0

Photographs © The Printer's Devil, except those on pages 32 (© Yes),
46 (© Stravaigin) and 49 (© Fratelli Sarti)

ISBN 0 00 472465-8

A catalogue record for this book is available from the British Library

Printed in Italy by Amadeus S.p.A.

# CONTENTS

## WHERE TO GO IN TOWN

## WHERE TO GO OUT OF TOWN

*The telephone code for Glasgow is 0141*

# INTRODUCTION

Welcome to the first edition of the new millennium of this city handbook extracted and updated from *Scotland the Best!* which, now in its fourth edition, has proven to be the most popular independent guide to our incredible country. Coming out every two years, it's the one the Scots use themselves, an insider guide written like this one by people who know and love their subject. Glasgow is a big subject: here it has been reduced and condensed so that only the good information is included. You should need no other guide, but please let us know what you think – we thrive on feedback.

As you become familiar with *Glasgow the Best!*, you will see that it is not quite like other guides. It doesn't give you lots of orientation information (it assumes you can negotiate your own arrival and can follow universal rules for survival in a new city) and you may need to consult a proper map (available free along with loads of other bumf from the Tourist Information Centres at the airport and in George Sq downtown) since our maps are very diagrammatic. What it does give you in a broad range of categories is the best of what Glasgow (and its immediate area) has to offer. We are highly selective and do not give all the options – only the best places. This includes the obvious, like the Burrell Collection, as well as the obscure, but nowhere is listed just because it's there – if it's mediocre, we ignore it. So, we're not too horrible about anyone – this is a positive book.

Although the selection process is undertaken by us, many people are consulted before choices are made and everywhere has been visited and sampled. We hope we are saving you the bother of having a less than satisfactory experience and we stand by all our recommendations. But nobody pays for inclusion, there are no ads, no subscriptions and no sponsorship. We do not employ a rigid set of standards and we tolerate idiosyncrasy because we'd rather have integrity and authenticity than mere amenity. Quality and attitude are what we recognize and want to bring to your attention. Service and atmosphere, attention to detail and value for money are all evaluated in making our decisions. This guide is written for you – not them – and not the 'industry'.

We want you to know that Glasgow is one of the best cities on earth.

Enjoy it!

# A DECLARATION OF FALLIBILITY

This guide is 'true', but it may not always be absolutely accurate. Since this may seem like a contradiction in terms, I should explain. *Glasgow the Best!* is a handbook of information about all the 'best' places in Glasgow. 'Best', you will understand, is a subjective term; it means 'best' according to what we think. Needless to say, there seem to be a lot of readers who agree with this judgement, and even if you don't you may see that I and my associates have gone to some efforts to reach our assertions. It's intended to be obvious that we are conveying opinions and impressions. They're true because the motives are true; we believe in what we are saying. We take no bribes and we have no vested interest in any of the places recommended, other than that we do talk things up and shamelessly proclaim the places we like or admire.

We hope it's plain where the facts end and the opinions begin. In guidebooks this is not always the case. However, it's with 'the facts' that inconsistencies may appear. We try to give accurate and clear directions explaining how to find a place and basic details that might be useful. This information is gleaned from a variety of sources and may be supplied by the establishment concerned. We do try to verify everything usually by visiting but things change and since nowhere we recommend has solicited their inclusion – we don't run copy past them – inaccuracies may occur. We hope that there aren't any, or many, but we may not find out until you let us know. We'd appreciate it if you would, so we can fix it for the next edition.

# HOW TO USE THIS BOOK

There are two ways to use this book:

1. There's a straightforward index at the back. If you know somewhere already (and it's any good) you should find it here. Numbers refer to page numbers.

2. The book can be used by categories, e.g. you can look up the best French restaurants or the best pubs with outdoor drinking. Each entry has an item number in the outside margin. These are in numerical order and allow easy cross-referencing.

   The categories are further divided up into groups, e.g. Where to Stay, Where to Eat. Each group has a map, on which are pinpointed the most important locations within the whole group, e.g. The Best Hotels. The maps cover the city centre only and are not to scale. They are intended to be diagrammatic only. Each entry has a map reference which can be found beneath the item number in the border. If an item is out of the centre, an arrow indicates its direction off the map. In the border this is denoted by an x, e.g. xD4 means 'Off the map at square D4'.

# TICKS FOR THE BEST THERE IS

Although everything listed in the book is notable and remarkable in some way, there are places that are outstanding even in this superlative company. Instead of marking them with a rosette or a star, they have been 'awarded' a tick, the symbol of the … the Best! guides.

 Among the very best in Scotland

 Among the best (of its type) in the UK

 Among the best (of its type) in the world, or simply unique

# A NOTE ON CATEGORIES

The book is arranged in five categories: Where to Stay; Where to Eat; Where to Drink; Where to Go (for general activities) in Town; and Where to Go out of Town. Within these five sections, categories range from the (mainly) very expensive, e.g. Best Hotels, to the fairly cheap, e.g. Best Hostels. The final section, Where to go out of Town, lists places near to the city, easily reached by car or public transport and for a range of interests. Like most of the other items in *Glasgow the Best!*, these have been extracted from *Scotland the Best!*, which covers the whole of the country.

## THE CODES

*1. The Item Code*

At the outside margin of every item is a code which will enable you to find it on a map. Thus **152** *D3* should be read as follows: **152** is the item number, listed in a simple consecutive order; *D3* is the map coordinate, to help pinpoint the item's location on the map grid. A coordinate such as *xE1* indicates that the item can be reached by leaving the map at grid reference *E1*.

*2. The Hotel Codes*

Below each hotel recommended is a band of codes as follows:

**20RMS   JAN-DEC   T/T   PETS   CC   KIDS   TOS   LOTS**

**20RMS**   means the hotel has 20 bedrooms in total. No differentiation is made as to the type of room. Most hotels will offer twin rooms as singles or put extra beds in doubles if required. This code merely gives an impression of size.

**JAN-DEC**   means the hotel is open all year round. APR-OCT means approximately from the beginning of April to the end of October.

**T/T**   refers to the facilities: T/ means there are direct-dial phones in the bedrooms, while /T means there are TVs in the bedrooms.

**PETS**   means the hotel accepts dogs and other pets, probably under certain conditions (e.g. pets should be kept in the bedroom). It's usually best to check first.

**XPETS**   indicates that the hotel does not generally accept pets.

**CC**   means the hotel accepts major credit cards (e.g. Access, Visa).

**XCC**   means the hotel does not accept major credit cards.

**KIDS**   indicates children are welcome and special provisions/rates may be available.

**XKIDS** does not necessarily mean that children are not able to accompany their parents, only that special provisions/rates are not usually made. Check by phone.

**TOS** means the hotel is part of the Taste of Scotland scheme and has been selected for having a menu which features imaginative cooking using Scottish ingredients. The Taste of Scotland produces an annual guide of members.

**LOTS** Rooms which cost more than £75 per night per person. The theory is that if you can afford over £150 a room, it doesn't matter too much if it's £160 or £175. Other price bands are:

**EXP** Expensive: £55-75 per person.

**MED.EXP** Medium (expensive): £45-55.

**MED.INX** Medium (inexpensive): £35-45.

**INX** Inexpensive: £25-35.

**CHP** Cheap: less than £25.

Rates are per person per night. They are worked out by halving the published average rate for a twin room in high season and should be used only to give an impression of cost. They are based on 2000 prices. Add between £2 and £5 per year, though the band should stay the same unless the hotel undergoes improvements.

*3. The Restaurant Code*

Found at the bottom right of all restaurant entries. It refers to the price of an average dinner per person with a starter, a main course and a dessert. It doesn't include wine, coffee or extras.

**EXP** Expensive: more than £40.

**MED** Medium: £25-40.

**INX** Inexpensive: £15-25.

**CHP** Cheap: less than £15.

These are based on 2000 rates. With inflation, the relative price bands should stay about the same.

*4. The Walk Codes*

A number of walks are described in the book. Below each walk is a band of codes as follows:

**2-10km CIRC BIKE 1-A-1**

**2-10km** means the walk(s) described may vary in length from 2km to 10km.

**CIRC** means the walk can be circular, while **XCIRC** shows the walk is not circular and you must return more or less by the way you came.

**BIKE** indicates the walk has a path which is suitable for ordinary bikes.

**XBIKE** means the walk is not suitable for, or does not permit, cycling.

**MTBIKE** means the track is suitable for mountain or all-terrain bikes.

The **1-A-1** Code

First number (**1, 2, 3**) indicates how easy the walk is.

**1** the walk is easy; **2** medium difficulty, e.g. standard hillwalking, not dangerous nor requiring special knowledge or equipment; **3** difficult: care, preparation and a map are needed.

The letters (**A, B, C**) indicate how easy it is to find the path.

A the route is easy to find. The way is either marked or otherwise obvious; B the route is not very obvious, but you'll get there; C you will need a map and preparation or a guide.

The last number (**1, 2, 3**) indicates what to wear on your feet.

**1** ordinary outdoor shoes, including trainers, are probably OK unless the ground is very wet; **2** you will need walking boots; **3** you will need serious walking or hiking boots.

Apart from the designated walks, the **1-A-1** code is employed wherever there is more than a short stroll required to get somewhere, e.g. a waterfall or a monument. The code appears at the bottom-right corner of the item.

# LIST OF ABBREVIATIONS

As well as codes and because of obvious space limitations, a personal short-hand and ad hoc abbreviation system has had to be created. I'm the first to admit some may be annoying, especially 'restau' for restaurant, but it's a long word and it comes up often. The others which are used are:

| | | | |
|---|---|---|---|
| accom | accommodation | incl | including |
| adj | adjacent | inexp | inexpensive |
| admn | admission | info | information |
| app | approach | jnct | junction |
| approx | approximately | L | loch |
| atmos | atmosphere | LO | last orders |
| av | average | min(s) | minute(s) |
| ave | avenue | N | north |
| AYR | all year round | no smk | no smoking |
| bedrms | bedrooms | nr | near |
| betw | between | NTS | National Trust for Scotland |
| br | bridge | | |
| BYOB | bring your own bottle | o/look(s) | overlook(s)/ing |
| cl | closes/closed | opp | opposite |
| cres | crescent | o/side | outside |
| dining-rm | dining-room | pl | place |
| dr | drive | poss | possible |
| E | east | pt | point/port |
| Edin | Edinburgh | R | river |
| esp | especially | r/bout | roundabout |
| excl | excluding | rd | road |
| exhib(s) | exhibition(s) | refurb | refurbished/ment |
| exp | expensive | restau | restaurant |
| facs | facilities | rm(s) | room(s) |
| ft | fort | rt | right |
| Glas | Glasgow | S | south |
| gr | great | sq | square |
| grd(s) | garden(s) | st | street |
| hr(s) | hour(s) | stn | station |
| HS | Historic Scotland | SYHA | Scottish Youth Hostels Association |

| | | | |
|---|---|---|---|
| terr | terrace | v | very |
| TO | tourist information office | vac | vacation |
| | | vegn | vegetarian |
| t/off | turn-off | W | west |
| trad | traditional | w/end(s) | weekend(s) |
| tratt | trattoria | yr(s) | year(s) |
| univ | university | | |

# WHERE TO STAY

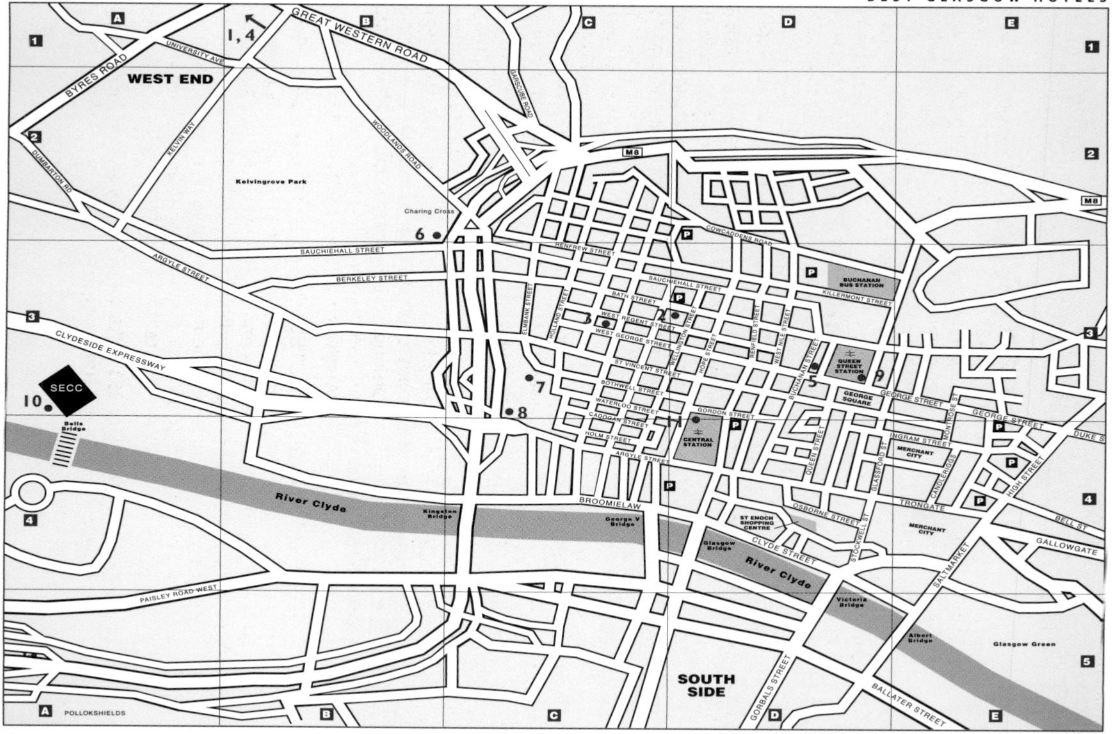
WEST END
BYRES ROAD
UNIVERSITY AVE
GREAT WESTERN ROAD
1, 4
GARSCUBE ROAD
WOODLANDS ROAD
KELVIN WAY
DUMBARTON RD
Kelvingrove Park
Charing Cross
6
M8
SAUCHIEHALL STREET
ARGYLE STREET
BERKELEY STREET
CLYDESIDE EXPRESSWAY
SECC
10
Bells Bridge
River Clyde
Kingston Bridge
PAISLEY ROAD WEST
POLLOKSHIELDS
7
8
ELMBANK STREET
HOLLAND STREET
RENFREW STREET
COWCADDENS ROAD
BATH STREET
WEST REGENT STREET
WEST GEORGE STREET
ST VINCENT STREET
BOTHWELL STREET
WATERLOO STREET
CADOGAN STREET
HOLM STREET
WELLINGTON STREET
HOPE STREET
RENFIELD STREET
WEST NILE STREET
BUCHANAN STREET
GORDON STREET
CENTRAL STATION
BROOMIELAW
George V Bridge
Glasgow Bridge
ST ENOCH SHOPPING CENTRE
CLYDE STREET
OSBORNE STREET
QUEEN STREET
BUCHANAN BUS STATION
KILLERMONT STREET
QUEEN STREET STATION
GEORGE SQUARE
GEORGE STREET
MONTROSE ST
INGRAM STREET
MERCHANT CITY
GLASSFORD ST
CANDLERIGGS
STOCKWELL ST
TRONGATE
HIGH STREET
DUKE S
BELL ST
GALLOWGATE
SALTMARKET
Victoria Bridge
Albert Bridge
Glasgow Green
GORBALS STREET
BALLATER STREET
SOUTH SIDE
1
2
3
4
5
9
P

**1**
*xB1*

✔✔✔**ONE DEVONSHIRE GARDENS:** 339 2001. 1 Devonshire Grds. Off Gr Western Rd (the A82 W to Dumbarton). After yrs at the front – it's still at the front. 3 separate houses in leafy Victorian terr, and after accolades and write-ups galore, remains the most notable urban hotel in Scotland. It's all down to detail and service, fab fixtures and fabrics: it's all down to DESIGN. Every rm is different but all have the things that we modern travellers look out for: CD players, big beds, deep baths, thick carpets/towels/curtains. Some Ralph Lauren rms; the supersuites all in house 3 (rms 21, 27, 28) if you're Pavarotti or just celebrating. Restau a foodie experience in itself (53/BEST RESTAUS). Stars aplenty – well it's the obvious choice. **27RMS JAN-DEC T/T PETS CC KIDS LOTS**

**2**
*D3*

✔**THE ARTHOUSE HOTEL:** 221 6789. 129 Bath St, nr Sauchiehall Centre and above Sarti (87/ITALIAN RESTAUS), so gr coffee downstairs. New (summer '99) and v smart town-house hotel with wide, tiled stairwell and funky lift to 3 floors of individual rms (so size, views, etc. vary). Fab gold-embossed wallpaper in the hallways, notable stained glass in 'fine' drawing-rm (The Arc) and nice pictures and prints. Grill downstairs has tepenyaki dishes and adj oyster bar. Chef John Quigley home at last. Bar, a fashionable rendezvous for this, the sexiest stopover in town. **68RMS JAN-DEC T/T XPETS CC KIDS MED.EXP**

**3**
*C3*

✔**MALMAISON:** 572 1000. 278 W George St. Sister hotel of the one in Edin and same team as One Devonshire (*see above*) so no surprise that this is an outstanding hotel. The 'chain' of good design hotel spread through England as we speak (dulcet tones of course). Café Mal downstairs contrasts with the woody clubbiness of the brasserie next door (68/BEST BISTROS). Well-proportioned rms (some suites), with CDs, cable, etc. Stylish excellence. This is indeed the Blair New World. **72RMS JAN-DEC T/T XPETS CC KIDS MED.EXP**

**4**
*xB1*

✔**THE DEVONSHIRE HOTEL:** 339 7878. 5 Devonshire Grds. Confusingly perhaps for first-time visitors, this similarly sumptuous town-house hotel is at the other end of the short block containing One Devonshire (*see above*). I say 'similarly' (pictures, plants, atmos, etc.), but it is less deluxe, less designey, some may find more easy on the pocket – and you don't have to be so cool. Dining for residents only. All bedrms different. **16RMS JAN-DEC T/T PETS CC KIDS LOTS**

**5**
*D3*

✔**CARLTON GEORGE:** 353 6373. 44 W George St. Adj Queen St Stn and George Sq, this is a smart new addition to Glas and apart from parking (a hike to carpark behind the stn) prob the best hotel in the city centre for the business traveller. It's more fun than that though, with a huge Irish bar downstairs and airy restau up top (mixed reviews). Residents' lounge and drinks in rm all on the house. Excellent service and the usual comforts.

**65RMS JAN-DEC T/T XPETS CC KIDS EXP**

**6**
*B2*

✓ **NAIRN'S:** 353 0707. 13 Woodside Cres, nr Charing Cross. 4 rms above Nick Nairn's eponymous restau and clearly one of the best places in town to have breakfast (and dinner) (50/BEST RESTAUS). Each rm v individual with different themes (one definitely more S&M than M&S), but all with good light and good bathrms.

**4RMS JAN-DEC T/T XPETS CC KIDS EXP**

**7**
*C4*

**GLASGOW HILTON:** 204 5555. 1 William St. App from the M8 slip rd or from city centre via Waterloo St. It has a forbidding Fritz Lang/*Metropolis* appearance which isn't really dispelled once inside. But this hotel is one of the best in town, with good service and appointments. Japanese people made esp welcome. Huge atrium. Cameron's, the hotel's main restau, is present and correct, and the most highly Michelin-rated restau in town ('99). Minsky's bistro and Raffles bar are not so special.

**319RMS JAN-DEC T/T PETS CC KIDS LOTS**

**8**
*C4*

**THE MARRIOTT:** 226 5577. 500 Argyle St, nr motorway. Modern and functional business hotel where parking is a test for the nerves. Nevertheless, there's a calm, helpful attitude from the staff inside; for further de-stressing you can hypnotize yourself by watching the soundless traffic on the Kingston Br o/side; or there's a pool to lap. No-smk floors.

**298RMS JAN-DEC T/T PETS CC KIDS LOTS**

**9**
*D3*

**THE COPTHORNE:** 332 6711. 50 George Sq. Situated on the sq which is the municipal heart of the city and next to Queen St Stn (trains to Edin and pts N), Glas will be going on all about you and there's a conservatory terr, serving breakfast and afternoon tea, from which to watch. Bedrms vary greatly; some perhaps overdone and over dear. Busy brasserie.

**141RMS JAN-DEC T/T PETS CC KIDS LOTS**

**10**
*A4*

**THE MOAT HOUSE:** 306 9988. Congress Rd. Beside the SECC, on the Clyde, this towering, glass monument to the 1980s feels like it's in a constant state of 'siege readiness'. The Marine Restau, in the lobby, has a good reputation and ring-side seating for river-gazing. Somewhat removed from city centre (about 3km, you wouldn't want to walk), it's esp handy for SECC and Armadillo.

**282RMS JAN-DEC T/T PETS CC KIDS LOTS**

**11**    **THE CENTRAL HOTEL:** 221 9680. Gordon St. Once the last word in gra-
*D3*    cious living, the elegance is now distinctly faded, although a certain
      atmos still remains in the sweep of the staircase and in the grandiose
      public rms. Rms are individual, though may be small (and too hot).
      Corridors stretch forever but you're at the hub of a gr city.

**221RMS JAN-DEC T/T PETS CC KIDS EXP**

Architectural splendour in St Vincent St

# THE BEST OF THE LESS EXPENSIVE HOTELS

**12**
*D3*
✓ ✓ **GROUCHO ST JUDES:** 352 8800. 190 Bath St. Late 20th-century collaboration betw Paul Wingate and Bobby Patterson of Glas and the Groucho Club of Soho. Downstairs bar, upstairs rms and good restau on ground floor. Urbane atmos throughout. Rms minimalist. Good rm service. Membership not required, just a bit of credential and credit card.
**6RMS JAN-DEC T/T XPETS CC XKIDS MED.EXP**

**13**
*E3*
✓ **CATHEDRAL HOUSE:** 552 3519. 28-32 Cathedral Sq/John Knox St. Next to the Cathedral (some rms o/look) and close to the Merchant City, this detached old building has been tastefully refurbed (though a redec may be due) and converted into a café-bar (with occasional live music), a separate restau (check opening though) and basic bedrms above. Discreet and informal hospitality for the traveller; much as it always has been here, in the ancient heart of the city.
**7RMS JAN-DEC T/T PETS CC KIDS MED.EXP**

**14**
*xB1*
✓ **THE TOWN HOUSE:** 357 0862. 4 Hughenden Terr. Quiet st off Gr Western Rd via Hyndland Rd, o/looking the cricket grounds. Spacious rms faithfully restored – even if you don't happen to live in a well-appointed town house on a gracious terr yourself, you'll feel at home. Close to the W End. Don't confuse with the Townhouse Hotel, Royal Cres.
**10RMS JAN-DEC T/T XPETS CC KIDS MED.INX**

**15**
*C3*
✓ **THE LODGE INN:** 221 1000. 10 Elmbank Grds, above Charing Cross Stn. Once an office block, then the Charing Cross Tower Hotel, this under new ownership (S&N) is still a vast city-centre budget hotel, with no frills and no pretence, but a v adequate rm for the night. Not a pile of charm and you wouldn't want to spend your holidays here, but its functionalism, anonymity and urban melancholy may suit the very modern traveller. M8 rms less quiet.
**276RMS JAN-DEC T/T XPETS CC KIDS MED.EXP**

**16**
*E4*
✓ **THE BRUNSWICK:** 552 0001. 104-108 Brunswick St. V contemporary, minimalist hotel in Merchant City. Bright and cheerful rms economically designed to make use of tight space; low Japanese-style beds. Good base for nocturnal forays into pub and club land. Restau has had mixed response, but breakfast v pleasant. Check out the penthouse.
**21RMS JAN-DEC T/T XPETS CC KIDS MED.EXP**

**17**
E4

✓ **RAB HA'S:** 572 0400. 83 Hutcheson St. Rms above a pub in the urban heart of the Merchant City that have had a recent overhaul. Good food and friendly folk make this a place to go if you're in the know. But noisy late night and if you lie in.  **4RMS JAN-DEC T/T PETS CC XKIDS MED.INX**

**18**
D4

✓ **THE MERCHANT LODGE HOTEL:** 552 2424. 52 Virginia St. Conversion of the old Tobacco Merchants house (in Merchant City) that has managed to retain the original staircase (ask the porter to take your bags, there's no lift). Surprisingly quiet area nr shops; in the gay zone (in case you didn't notice).  **34RMS JAN-DEC T/T PETS CC KIDS CHP**

**19**
D4, D3

**HOLIDAY INN EXPRESS:** 0800 897121. Corner of Stockwell and Clyde St (but you don't get a room on the river). Functional bed-box that's still a good deal. All you do is sleep here. Nr Merchant City, so plenty of restaus, nightlife and other distractions and curiously midway betw 2 of Glasgow's oldest, funkiest bars – The Scotia and Victoria (203/202/GR GLAS PUBS). Another branch (88rms) on corner of W Nile St at Cowcaddens (331 6800) – same concept and proportions. Similarly, no restau but **PRONTO** adj is handy for morning cappuccino.  **120RMS JAN-DEC T/T XPETS CC KIDS MED.INX**

**20**
E4

**BABBITY BOWSTER:** 552 5055. 16-18 Blackfriars St. This carefully reno-vated, late 18th-century town house was pivotal in the redevelopment of the Merchant City. Renowned for its hospitality; bar (224/REAL-ALE PUBS, 337/PUB FOOD) and beer grd (251/DRINK OUTDOORS), Schottische restau upstairs and simple accom above. A welcoming howf, some Culture thrown in, a basic rm.  **6RMS JAN-DEC X/X XPETS CC XKIDS MED.INX**

**21**
xA2

**WICKETS HOTEL:** 334 9334. 52 Fortrose St. Probably best app via Dumbarton Rd, turning up Peel St before railway br. O/looking W of Scotland Cricket Ground, family-run hotel with decent rms, conservatory restau and a beer grd made for long summer afternoons (249/DRINK OUT-DOORS).  **10RMS JAN-DEC T/T PETS CC KIDS MED.INX**

**22**
xA1

**KIRKLEE:** 334 5555. 11 Kensington Gate. The Stevens keep a tidy house and most notably a tidy grd in this leafy suburb nr Botanics and Byres Rd.  **9RMS JAN-DEC T/T XPETS CC KIDS MED.INX**

**23**
xA1

**THE WHITE HOUSE:** 339 9375. 12 Cleveden Cres. Not really a hotel, more self-catering apartments nr Botanics. V civilized alternative, esp if there are a few of you or you are staying a week. Nightly lets, cool place.  **6UNITS JAN-DEC T/T PETS CC KIDS MED.INX**

**24**  **NUMBER 52 CHARLOTTE STREET:** 553 1941. Serviced apartments in
*E4*  superb conversion of the one remaining Georgian town house in historic
(now decimated) st betw the Barrows Market and Glas Green. V good
rates for bedrm/lounge/kitchen; everything but breakfast.

**6RMS JAN-DEC X/T XPETS CC KIDS MED.INX**

**25**  **THEATRE HOTEL:** 227 2772. 27 Elmbank St. The theatre is the Kings in
*C3*  the W End; this reasonably appointed budget hotel is just down the
(rather bleak) road. But it is OK inside, better than most and inexp. No
dining-rm ('continental breakfast' served in your rm). But there's 'a wide
variety of eating places nearby', as they say.

**59RMS JAN-DEC T/T PETS CC KIDS MED.INX**

**26**  **THE VICTORIAN HOUSE:** 332 0129. 214 Renfrew St. Expansive guest-
*C3*  house which has swallowed up adj houses in hill-top terr behind
Sauchiehall St nr Art School (309/MACKINTOSH). Basic accom. Rms without
facs cheaper but bathrms can be a floor away. Location is the appeal.

**55RMS JAN-DEC X/T PETS CC KIDS INX**

**27**  **RENNIE MACKINTOSH HOTEL:** 333 9992. 218-220 Renfrew St and the
*C2, B3*  **GREEK THOMSON:** 332 6556, 140 Elderslie St, have both cheekily bor-
rowed the names of 2 of Glasgow's most famous sons. The Mockintosh
isn't too overbearing, the service is friendly and helpful, and there's alfresco breakfasting in the summer.

**24/17RMS JAN-DEC T/T X/PETS CC KIDS INX**

# THE BEST HOSTELS

*The SYHA is the Scottish Youth Hostel Association, of which you have to be a member (or a member of an affiliated organization from another country) to stay in their many hostels round Scotland. Phone 01786 451181 for details, or contact any YHA hostel.*

**28**
*B2*
✓ **SY HOSTEL:** 332 3004. 7 Park Terr. Close to where the old Glas hostel used to be in Woodlands Terr, in the same area of the W End nr the univ and Kelvingrove Park. This building was converted in 1992 from the Beacons Hotel, which was where rock 'n' roll bands used to stay in the 1980s. Now the bedrms are converted into dorms for 4-6 (some larger) and the public rms are common rms with TV, games, café, etc. Still feels more like a hotel than a hostel and is a gr place to stay.       **160BEDS**

**29**
*B2*
✓ **GLASGOW BACKPACKERS:** 332 9099. 17 Park Terr. Along from the SYH (*see above*), the funkier alternative. Mostly dorms but some twins available. Only open summer months. Close to W End.       **92BEDS**

**30**
*C3*
✓ **BAIRD HALL, STRATHCLYDE UNIV:** 553 4148. 460 Sauchiehall St. The landmark Grade A-listed Art Deco building near the Art School and the W End. Originally the Beresford Hotel, built 1937 and once Glasgow's finest (v Miami Beach). 194 rms in vacs and 11 available AYR. Spartan, almost drab, though the rms are fine, like an American Y. Reeks of nostalgia as well as disinfectant. Dining-rm, TV and reading rm. Lots of groovy places nearby such as Bar Ce Lona, Variety Bar, Baby Grand and the Griffin. All are listed further on.       **185BEDS**

**31**
*D4*
**CLYDE HALL, STRATHCLYDE UNIV:** 553 4148 318. Clyde St. A v central block, off-campus at the bottom of Union/Renfield St and almost o/looking the river. 165 single and twin rms, mainly in summer vac. Refectory and TV rm. Some smaller rms on lower floor are available cheaply as self-catering specifically for backpackers, and are a v good deal.       **128BEDS**

**32**
*E3*
**MURRAY HALL, STRATHCLYDE UNIV:** 553 4148 (ext 3560). Collins St. Modern, but not sterile block of single rms on edge of main campus and facing towards Cathedral. Part of large complex (also some student flats to rent by the week) with bar/shop/laundrette. Quite central, close to Merchant City bars. Vacs only.       **70BEDS**

*Note: Both Strathclyde and Glas univs have other halls available for short-term accom in the summer. For those above and others, you may also phone: Glas 330 5385 or Strathclyde 553 4148 (central booking).*

# THE BEST CAMPING AND CARAVAN PARKS

*Refer to Around Glasgow map on pages 116–17.*

**33**
**E3**
**STRATHCLYDE PARK:** 01698 266155. 20km SE of Glas. M74 at jnct 6 or M8/A725. On the edge of a large popular country park and easily reached by the motorway system. Go left just after park entrance. Check in until 9.30pm. Stay up to 2 weeks. Usual but good standard facs on site and many others nearby, e.g. café, windsurfing, gym till 8.30pm, 500m away. Motorway close, so traffic noise, but no visual intrusion on this well-managed parkland site. Caravans and tents separate. Glasgow's most accessible caravan park by car. 250 pitches. Apr-Oct. (386/O/SIDE GLAS)

**34**
**C3**
**BARNBROCK, LOCHWINNOCH:** 01505 614791. 40km SW of Glas via M8/A8 Pt Glas then Kilmacolm rd A761, then B786; or via Johnstone on A737, A760 to Lochwinnoch. Let's face it, it's not exactly convenient, but this beautiful, remote site (camping only) is on the edge of the wild and wonderful Muirshiel Country Park and Lochwinnoch Nature Reserve, and it's not far to go to leave the city behind completely. 15 tents. (387/O/SIDE GLAS)

**35**
**C3**
**CLOCH CARAVAN PARK, GOUROCK:** 01475 632675. 45km W of Glas along the coast. Take M8 then A8 through Greenock and Gourock; continue for 6km. Residential caravan park (no tents) with only a few touring pitches. Best feature is that it o/looks the historical Cloch Pt Lighthouse and the R Clyde. 10 places only.

**36**
**D2**
**TULLICHEWAN, BALLOCH:** 01389 759475. 40km NW of Glas. A fair distance from the city, but fast rds in this direction via A82 (dual carriageway all the way), or via Erskine Br and then M8. Best to leave the car here and take frequent train service from Balloch Stn nearby; 30mins to Glas Central Stn. This park is nicely situated nr L Lomond and tourist centres, and is well managed and good fun for kids. Shop, laundrette, games rm, TV, sauna, sunbeds, etc. Probably the best park for holiday-making hereabouts. 140 places.

**37**
**C2**
**ARDLUI, LOCH LOMOND:** 01301 704243. Continue on A82 (*from above*). At the other end of the loch in an ideal spot for exploring by boat (they have hiring facs and a 100 berth marina) or on foot. For self-catering, 6-8 berth caravans are available and there's an on-site hotel (11 rms, 2 bars and 2 restaus) if your tent blows away in the night. Laundry, children's play area, shop. 97 places.

# THE BEST HOTELS OUTSIDE TOWN

*Refer to Around Glasgow map on pages 116–17.*

**38**
*C3*
✓ **GLEDDOCH HOUSE, LANGBANK, nr GREENOCK:** 01475 540711. Take M8/A8 to Greenock, then B789 signposted Langbank/Houston, then 2km – hotel is signed. 30km W of centre by fast rd. A château-like country-house hotel, formerly the home of the Lithgow shipping family. High above the Clyde estuary, there are spectacular views across to Dumbarton Rock and the Kilpatrick Hills. Rms not lavish but comfortable – only a few have the view. Reputable dining-rm strong on Scottish ingredients and cuisine. Pleasant conservatory. Excellent 18-hole golf course (297/SPORTS FACS); health club, tiny pool.
**38RMS JAN-DEC T/T PETS CC KIDS TOS LOTS**

**39**
*D2*
✓ **CAMERON HOUSE, nr BALLOCH, LOCH LOMOND:** 01389 755565. A82 dual carriageway through W End or via Erskine Br and M8. 45km NW of centre. Highly regarded mansion-house hotel complex with excellent leisure facs in open grounds on the bonny banks of the loch. Sports incl 9-hole golf, good pool, tennis and a busy marina for sailing/windsurfing, etc. Notable restau (The Georgian Rm) and all-day brasserie. Many famous names from Gazza to Pavarotti have holed up here (but they wouldn't have Oasis).
**96RMS JAN-DEC T/T XPETS CC KIDS TOS LOTS**

**40**
*D2*
✓ **THE BLACK BULL HOTEL, KILLEARN:** 01360 550215. 2 The Sq. A81 towards Aberfoyle, take the rt fork after Glengoyne Distillery, and the hotel is at the top end of the village next to the church. Open-plan bar/restau with excellent reputation for food (2 AA rosettes), spacious conservatory with enclosed grd, and tastefully decorated, comfortable rms. (404/O/SIDE GLAS)   **11RMS JAN-DEC T/T PETS CC KIDS MED.EXP**

**41**
*D4*
✓ **NEW LANARK MILL HOTEL, LANARK:** 01555 667200. From Glas, take M74, then follow signs for Lanark and esp New Lanark, the conservation village of Robert Owen (45 mins). Excellent retreat from Glas, where you wake up on the banks of the Clyde and sleep to the sound of its running water. Serene spot though many visitors. Good walks up river (385/O/SIDE GLAS) and an excellent restau in Lanark (10 mins), La Vigna (406/O/SIDE GLAS).   **38RMS JAN-DEC T/T PETS CC KIDS MED.INX**

**42**
**D4** ✓ **SCORETULLOCH HOUSE HOTEL, DARVEL:** 01560 323331. M74, jnct 8 for A71 Kilmarnock. Signed and 2km from rd E of Priestland nr Darvel. On a hillside o/looking the R Irvine. An unimposing country house with notable restaus – Loudoun Rm for imaginative fine dining (2 AA rosettes) and Oscar's Brasserie. Go-for-it attitude here (they even have a newsletter) and gr attention to comfort and detail. Good hideaway from Glas (they say, 30 mins up the rd).
**29RMS JAN-DEC T/T PETS CC KIDS MED.INX**

**43**
**D2** ✓ **THE LODGE ON LOCH LOMOND:** 01436 860201. Edge of Luss on A82 N from Balloch. About 40 mins from W End. Linear not lovely, but gr lochside setting. Wood-lined rms o/look the bonny banks, though Luss is not everybody's cup of tea (and sausage roll). Restau also has the view and terr and is surprisingly good – AA rosette; booking may be necessary w/ends.
**29RMS JAN-DEC T/T PETS CC KIDS MED.INX**

**44**
**D3** **COUNTRY CLUB HOTEL, STRATHBLANE:** 01360 770491. 20km N and only 20mins from Maryhill Rd on a good day (follow A81, the Milngavie rd, to Strathblane). Not new (refurbed '97), but fresh outlook. A civilized lodging to N of city with good restau (1 AA rosette) and more informal brasserie. Rms individual, reasonably well appointed; carefully chosen pictures.
**10RMS JAN-DEC T/T PETS CC KIDS EXP**

**45**
**D3** **BOTHWELL BRIDGE HOTEL, BOTHWELL:** 01698 852246. Uddingston t/off from M74, 15km SE of centre. Main St. Nr castle (379/O/SIDE GLAS) and pub (213/'UNSPOILT' PUBS). Comfortable, family-run hotel with an Italian ambience. V kid-friendly.
**90RMS JAN-DEC T/T XPETS CC KIDS EXP**

**46**
**D2** **CULCREUCH CASTLE HOTEL, FINTRY:** 01360 860555. Off B818 in Campsie Fells, 32km N of centre via A81 Milngavie rd from Glas. Fintry is well kept and in a valley betw the Fells and the Fintry Hills. Some fine walking (364/WALKS O/SIDE THE CITY). Ancestral home of the Galbraiths with many old features, incl a half-tester bed. Dungeons converted into bar/bistro. Many weddings, so check w/ends.
**8RMS JAN-DEC T/T PETS CC KIDS TOS MED.INX**

**47**
**C3** **THE INVERKIP HOTEL, INVERKIP:** 01475 521478. M8 from Glas then A8 and A78 from Pt Glas heading S for Largs. 50km W of centre. Inverkip is a wee bypassed village now dominated from the other side of the main rd by the Kip Marina (400/O/SIDE GLAS). Hotel is in Main St; a family-run coaching inn with busy pub downstairs. The most reasonable place to stay on this part of the Clyde coast.
**6RMS JAN-DEC X/T PETS CC KIDS INX**

**48** **KIRKTON HOUSE, CARDROSS:** 01389 841951. Darleith Rd. A814, past
C3  Helensburgh to Cardross village then N up Darleith Rd. Kirkton House is
1km on rt. 18th-century Scottish farmhouse that combines rustic charm
with *every* mod con (check your web site). Informal and unpretentious
('no hang-ups'), quality home-cooking and a stone's throw from L
Lomond. International clientele.

**6RMS FEB-NOV T/T PETS CC KIDS MED.INX**

**BAIRD HALL** 'landmark Grade A-listed Art Deco building' (page 21)

# WHERE TO EAT

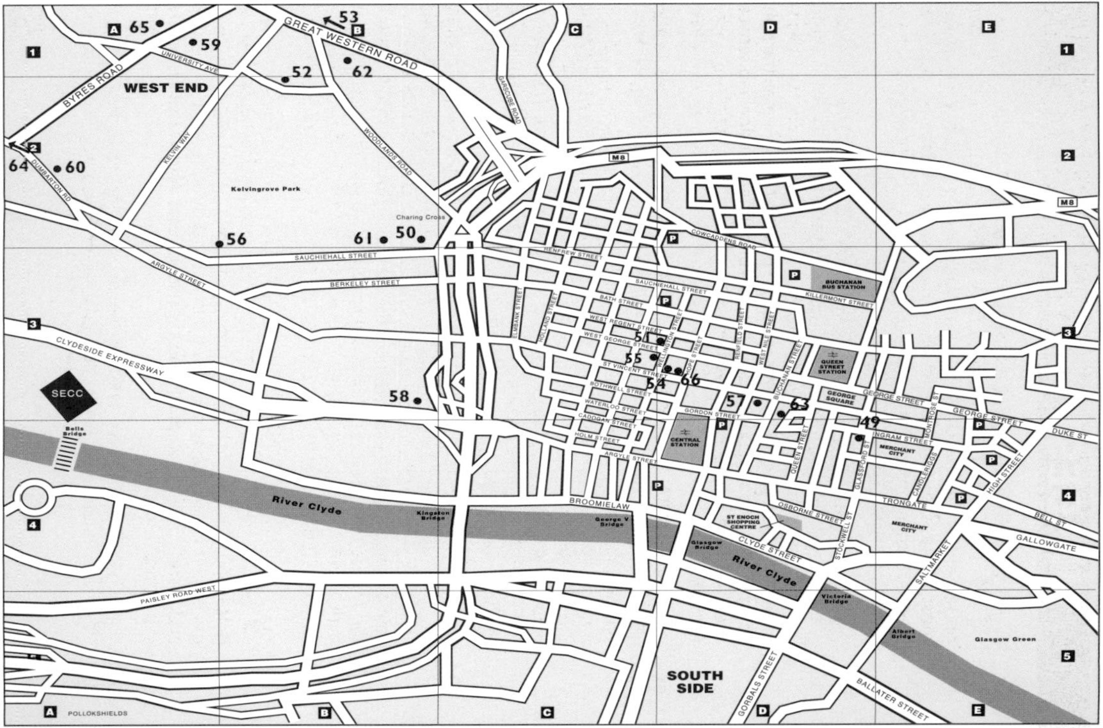
WEST END
GREAT WESTERN ROAD
BYRES ROAD
UNIVERSITY AVE
DUMBARTON RD
KELVIN WAY
WOODLANDS ROAD
GARSCUBE ROAD
Kelvingrove Park
Charing Cross
SAUCHIEHALL STREET
ARGYLE STREET
BERKELEY STREET
CLYDESIDE EXPRESSWAY
SECC
Bells Bridge
River Clyde
Kingston Bridge
George V Bridge
Glasgow Bridge
Victoria Bridge
Albert Bridge
PAISLEY ROAD WEST
POLLOKSHIELDS
SOUTH SIDE
GORBALS STREET
BALLATER STREET
Glasgow Green
SALTMARKET
GALLOWGATE
BELL ST
HIGH STREET
DUKE ST
TRONGATE
MERCHANT CITY
STOCKWELL ST
CLYDE STREET
OSBORNE STREET
ST ENOCH SHOPPING CENTRE
BROOMIELAW
M8
COWCADDENS ROAD
RENFREW STREET
BUCHANAN BUS STATION
KILLERMONT STREET
BATH STREET
WEST REGENT STREET
WEST GEORGE STREET
ST VINCENT STREET
BOTHWELL STREET
WATERLOO STREET
CADOGAN STREET
HOLM STREET
GORDON STREET
CENTRAL STATION
ELMBANK STREET
HOLLAND STREET
WELLINGTON STREET
HOPE STREET
RENFIELD STREET
WEST NILE STREET
BUCHANAN STREET
QUEEN STREET STATION
GEORGE SQUARE
GEORGE STREET
MONTROSE ST
INGRAM STREET
QUEEN STREET
GLASSFORD ST
CANDLERIGGS
P
A B C D E
1 2 3 4 5
49 50 51 52 53 54 55 56 57 58 59 60 61 62 63 64 65 66

**49**
**D4**  ✓ ✓ **CORINTHIAN:** 552 1107. 191 Ingram St. Beautiful restau in a fabulous Merchant City building nr George Sq (and GOMA). Bars on same floor (200/GR GLAS PUBS) and 'members' club' above, but restau most impressive part. Vaulted rm in immaculate condition could be Vienna. Contemporary British menu and good service – wines exp. 7 days. Cl Sat lunch. LO 10pm. **MED**

**50**
**B2**  ✓ ✓ **NAIRN'S:** 353 0707. 13 Woodside Cres, nr Charing Cross. Ubiquitous telly chef Nick Nairn's notable and first Glas venture (another restau imminent at going to press) on 2 floors in this W End town house (accom in 4 rms upstairs – 6/BEST HOTELS). Hits all the right spots in urban contemporary dining – smart, confident cuisine and service. You'd be hard put to find anywhere else of this quality at these prices. *Michelin Bib Gourmand '99.* **MED**

**51**
**C3**  ✓ ✓ **GAMBA:** 572 0899. 225a W George St. Mellow minimalist seafood restau in basement at corner of W Campbell St. Brave opposition in the seafood stakes to Two Fat Ladies (*see below*) in a city more inclined to the other steaks, but owner Alan Tomkins of Papingo (70/BEST BISTROS) knows exactly what he's doing and, as expected, the wine list is well chosen. Fashionable foodie choice for '99 and winner of the Highland Spring Restaurant of the Year. Lunch and dinner. LO 10.30pm. Cl Sun. (141/SEAFOOD RESTAUS) **MED**

**52**
**B2**  ✓ ✓ **STRAVAIGIN:** 334 2665. 28-30 Gibson St. Constantly changing, innovative and consciously eclectic menu from award-winning chef Colin Clydesdale. Mixes cuisines, esp Asian and Pacific Rim. Pleasant café-bar upstairs is more continental. Excellent, affordable food without the foodie formalities and open later than most. One of 2 Glas restaus with 3 AA rosettes '99 (other is One Devonshire Gardens). Mon-Thu 12noon-12midnight, Fri-Sat 12noon-1am, Sun 5pm-12midnight. **INX**

**53**
**xB1**  ✓ ✓ **ONE DEVONSHIRE GARDENS:** 339 2001. Glasgow's most stylish hotel (1/BEST HOTELS) has a restau which has won accolades in its own rt. Like the sumptuous surroundings, dishes on the fixed-price menu are contemporary, voguish and seductive. Staff are young and friendly. All in all, a smart food experience that doesn't feel like you're in a hotel. **EXP**

**54**
**D3**  ✓ ✓ **EURASIA:** 204 1150. St Vincent St. One of Scotland's most notable chefs, Ferrier Richardson (also of Yes *below*) opened this

stylish fusion restau in late '99. Minimalist, corporate feel, so many suits (who can afford the tab). **EXP**

**55**
*C3*
✔ **ROCOCO:** 221 5004. 202 W George St. Corner of Wellington St and just along from Bouzy Rouge to which it is related (86/BEST BISTROS). But this is the upmarket, fine dining and impeccable service version. Excellent contemporary menu has the lot in the mix. Nice private dining area and smokers courtyard o/side for post-prandial chat and coffee. Lunch and LO 10.30pm. Cl Sun. **EXP**

**56**
*A3*
✔ **AIRORGANIC:** 564 5201. 36 Kelvingrove St. Much-applauded, media-friendly bar/café and upstairs restau in the former Bar Miro. Proprietor Colin McDougal and designer Dene Happell have created an airy and stylish ambience for the purposefully organic bar and cuisine. This includes beer and wine list, bar snacks and a full menu upstairs. All as organic as poss. Menu not vegn – does include meat and fish. Bar: food LO 9pm. Restau LO 11pm, 12midnight w/ends. (233/PUB FOOD) **INX**

**57**
*D3*
✔ **YES:** 221 8044. 22 W Nile St. Downtown and downstairs (though street-level café-bar is a good place to meet and the 'Express Menu' one of the best-value light meals in town) is the airy and uncluttered creation of Ferrier Richardson. Some Asian/Pacific influence to superbly balanced dishes presented with flair and no fuss. Lunch and LO 11pm (upstairs 9pm). Both cl Sun. **MED**

**58**
*B3*
✔ **THE BUTTERY:** 221 8188. 652 Argyle St. Central but curious location for Glasgow's most consistently superb restau owned, as is the Rogano (*see below*), by Alloa Breweries. Occupying the only remaining tenement block in an area carved up by urban developers, the Buttery and its little brother downstairs, The Belfry (80/BEST BISTROS), are best reached via the westerly extension of St Vincent St then Elderslie St. Comfortable old-fashioned elegance will probably outlive most of the makeovers in these pages. Don't miss the winning sample-all-desserts option. 6 days, lunch and 7-10pm. Cl Sun and Sat lunch. **EXP**

**59**
*A1*
✔ **THE UBIQUITOUS CHIP:** 334 5007. 12 Ashton Lane. A cornerstone of culinary Glas. 2-storey, covered courtyard draped with vines, off a bar-strewn cobbled lane in the heart of the W End, heaped with accolades over 27 yrs in residence. The main bit is still one of the most atmospheric of rms. The menu is exemplary Scottish seafood, the best of seafood, game and beef and fine, original cooking. An outstanding wine list. Chip upstairs is cheaper. (84/BEST BISTROS). Daily lunch and 6.30-11pm. **EXP**

**60**
*A2* ✓ **TWO FAT LADIES:** 339 1944. 88 Dumbarton Rd, along from Kelvingrove Museum nr the end of Byres Rd. Calum Mathieson's long-established seafood bistro still takes the best line on fish in the city. Easy on the eye and palate (nothing too fancy) and for this degree of integrity and reliability, easy on the pocket. Simply sound. Tue-Sat LO 10pm, lunch Fri-Sat only. Cl Sun. (141/SEAFOOD RESTAUS) **MED**

**61**
*B2* ✓ **THAI FOUNTAIN:** 332 2599. 2 Woodside Cres, Charing Cross. Same ownership as Amber Regent (*see below*), this is probably Glasgow's best Asian restau. Genuinely Thai and not at all Chinese. Innovative dishes with gr diversity of flavours and textures, so sharing several is best. Of course you will eat too much. Cl Sun. (115/FAR-EASTERN RESTAUS) **MED**

**62**
*B1* ✓ **LA PARMIGIANA:** 334 0686. 447 Gr Western Rd. Simply the best Italian for many discriminating Glaswegians (convenient location nr Kelvin Br – usually parking nearby), the favourite posh place to eat without the ceremony and dulcet tones. Contemporary, perhaps predictable, cuisine. For when you can't face anything that isn't lightly done in olive oil. LO 11pm. Cl Sun. (88/ITALIAN RESTAUS) **MED**

**63**
*D4* ✓ **ROGANO:** 248 4055. 11 Exchange Pl. Betw Buchanan St and Queen St. An institution in Glas since the 1930s. Décor replicating a Cunard ship, the *Queen Mary*, is the major attraction. *The* place to take visiting friends or clients, even if just for cocktails. Restau spacious, perennially fashionable, with fish and seafood the specialities. Downstairs has a lighter/cheaper menu, and though a bit sub-Rogano its informality is easier on the pocket. Restaurant: lunch and 6-10.30pm. Café Rogano: lunch and 6-11pm (Fri-Sat until 12midnight, Sun until 10pm). **EXP.MED**

**64**
*xA2* **THE CABIN:** 569 1036. 996 Dumbarton Rd. Beautifully cooked fresh seafood and Scottish game, home-made Irish soda bread and delicious puds. You'll probably have to linger after dinner, when Wilma, legendary waitress and *chanteuse*, does her diva thing. A Glas original. BYOB if you like. Check by phone for lunch, Wed-Sat dinner. LO 9pm (w/end booked far in advance). **MED**

**65**
*A1* **PUPPET THEATRE:** 339 8444. 11 Ruthven Lane. In a converted mews behind Byres Rd, one of Scotland's most stylish restaus. Intimate dining areas; the crescent-shaped conservatory is the most popular and may be tightly packed. Fixed-price menus. Contemporary British with Scottish slant. Lunch (not Sat); LO 10.30pm. Cl Mon. **EXP**

**66** **BUDDA:** 243 2212. 142 St Vincent St. Downstairs bar with N African slant
*D3*  and this atmospheric restau behind the drapes at the back. Good fusion
cooking with all the right contemporary references. Mon-Sat lunch and
LO 10.30pm. Sun dinner only. **INX**

**AMBER REGENT:** 50 W Regent St. Report: 119/FAR-EASTERN RESTAUS.

**KILLERMONT POLO CLUB:** 2002 Maryhill Rd. Report: 105/INDIAN
RESTAUS.

**YES** 'superbly balanced dishes presented with flair
and no fuss' (page 30)

**67**
B3, A1

✓ **MITCHELLS:** 204 4312. 2 branches, both W. 157 N St on the left bank of M8 at the Mitchell Library, next to the Bon Accord (221/REAL-ALE PUBS). Ales here too, but notably *the* place for informal and v good food with a genuine bistro atmos. Intimate, more colourful version in busy Ashton Lane off Byres Rd (339 2220) has helpful BYOB, inx pre-theatre menu and more laid-back atmos. Both have food until 11pm, bar till 12midnight. Cl Sun. **INX**

**68**
C3

✓ **MALMAISON:** 221 6401. 278 W George St. The brasserie in the basement of the hotel (3/BEST HOTELS) with the same setup in Edin and a v similar menu. Excellent brasserie ambience in meticulously designed woody salon. Seating layout and busy waiters mean lots of buzz; also private dining-rms and the adjacent **CAFÉ MAL** in bright contrast. Fixed-menu lunch or dinner Mediterranean style with daily specials. 7 days, lunch and LO 10.30pm. **MED**

**69**
D3

✓ **ARTHOUSE GRILL:** 572 6002. 129 Bath St. Basement restau of excellent Arthouse Hotel (2/BEST HOTELS); enter through fab foyer or off st. Telly chef John Quigley presides over brasserie-type menu, incl lots of seafood and simple meat dishes alongside genuine (sit-round) tepanyaki grill. Sometimes food is not most fab, but expectations are high here. Always good atmos. 7 days lunch and dinner. LO 10/10.30pm. **INX**

**70**
D3

✓ **PAPINGO:** 332 6678. 104 Bath St. Bright bistro in a cool basement an enduring success story and still feels … well good enough to eat. The food is Scottish/French and perfectly portioned, esp for pre-theatre dinner. Wines and waiters are esp well chosen. A smooth operation! Daily till 10.30/11pm. **INX**

**71**
C3

✓ **BABY GRAND:** 248 4942. 3-7 Elmbank Grds. Inviting haven among high-rise office blocks opp hotel (15/LESS EXP HOTELS); a downtown-USA location. (Go behind the King's Theatre down Elmbank St, rt at gas stn and look for the hotel.) Narrow rm with bar stools and banquettes, often with background music from resident mad pianist. Light, eclectic menu from tapas to full meals materialize in the tiny gantry. Daily 8am-12midnight/1am. **CHP**

**72**
D3

✓ **GROUCHO ST JUDES:** 352 8800. 190 Bath St. Ground floor restau/bistro of the hotel (12/LESS EXP HOTELS) outpost of the Soho hostelry we've all read about. Not so bohemian rhapsody and no sign of Robbie Coltrane or Williams, but a fairly stylish station on the far northern line. Almost excludes anyone who isn't self-important somehow. Fortunately there's a lot of us. Menu contemporary British and fine at that. Bar menu downstairs lighter and inexp is a v good bet – pastas, mainly vegn, sandwiches and mains, incl fish 'n' chips. Choice puds. Bar all day till 8pm. Restau lunch Mon-Fri, dinner 7 days. LO 10.30pm. **INX.EXP**

**73**
*A2*
✔ **NO. SIXTEEN:** 339 2544. 16 Byres Rd. The current W End fave for dinner *à deux*. Tiny restau at the tackier end of Byres Rd in a site that has seen many menus. Now at last a winning combo – good bistro food, no fuss and inx. Sublime puds. Lunch and LO 10pm. Cl Sun. Best book! **INX**

**74**
*D4*
**BIER HALLE REPUBLIC:** 204 0706. 9 Gordon St. 130 beers in a concrete vault on Gordon St off Buchanan St. This is the latest creation of Colin Barr (originally The Living Room, The Tunnel and The Apartment – 243/THESE ARE HIP, 359/360/THE BEST CLUBS). Surprisingly, also good for food of the comfort variety, e.g. stews, goulash and things that go with drinking. Student atmos. 7 days, 12noon-7pm; bar till 12midnight. **CHP**

**75**
*D4*
**BLUE BAR CAFÉ:** The Lighthouse, Mitchell Lane. The first Glas venture of Andrew Radford and intended to be a replica of his highly-regarded Edin café/bar of the same name. At time of going to press, moving towards more flexible food available all day but afternoon and early evening lighter menus. Also developing bar side (with DJ nights) à la Bar 10 opp (207/GR GLASGOW PUBS). 7 days till 12midnight. LO 11pm. **THE DOOCOT**, an organic café and bar by the people who brought us Antipasti (93/ITALIAN RESTAUS), is on the top floor of The Lighthouse (313/MACKINTOSH). More fashion than food. Same hrs as Blue. **INX**

**76**
*xA1*
**COTTIER'S:** 357 5827. 93 Hyndland Rd. Off the top of Hyndland St nr Highburgh Rd. Converted church that encompasses a bar; regular live music (258/LIVE MUSIC) and benches o/side, a restau with an interesting menu made up of light, spicy dishes and a theatre that stages a broad range of music throughout the yr. A v broad church. (187/SUN BREAKFAST and other references.) 7 days. **INX**

**77**
*A2*
**JANSSENS:** 334 9682. 1355 Argyle St opp Kelvingrove Art Gallery. I missed it out last time and hundreds of people complained. OK, you go there, you like it – it's unpretentious, gr atmos (esp at night). You feel safe. It's because I'm not Glaswegian, it's because oops … I've never been there. Now I have. OK, I agree. It's in the book. 7 days 12noon-late. **INX**

**78** **ESCA:** 553 0880. 27 Chisholm St, opp Tron Theatre off Argyle St. A bright
*E4* new restau serving Italian dishes with a contemporary twist, particularly
fish and seafood, as well as the tried and tested pasta and pizza. 7 days,
lunch and 5-11pm. **CHP**

**79** **STAZIONE:** 576 7576. 1057 Gr Western Rd. Nr Gartnavel Hospital, which
*xB1* for non-Glaswegians means a long way down Gr Western Rd from the
Botanics corner. Informal bar/bistro bit of the rather more formal **LUX**
(upstairs). Mediterranean/Italian, relaxed ambience. O/side tables in summer. 7days, lunch and 5-11pm. **INX**

**80** **THE BELFRY:** 221 0630. 652 Argyle St. App via W extension of St Vincent
*B3* St, Elderslie St and left at the conical church. The basement of the Buttery,
one of Glasgow's finest restaus (58/BEST RESTAUS), in the one remaining
tenement of an area savaged by the M8. Bistro version of the
Scots/French cuisine served up top, in study-like cellar rms with dark
wood and books. Mon-Sat lunch, 6-11pm. Cl Sun.

**81** **LOOP:** 572 1472. 64 Ingram St, Merchant City. Main Rd for traffic nr
*E4* Fruitmarket venue. Contemporary café-restau, light and stylish design.
Seems like there's a lot like this in Glas, but Loop may last. From risotto to
bangers and mash, so hits most of the now buttons. We shall see (you
there). 7 days, 11am – LO 10.30pm. **MED**

**82** **CUL DE SAC:** 334 8899. 44 Ashton Lane, the main lane off Byres Rd with
*A1* the Grosvenor Cinema (319/NIGHTLIFE) and The Ubiquitous Chip (59/BEST
RESTAUS). Perennially fashionable crêperie/diner dedicated to serving
good, simple food with flair, even wit. The atmos is relaxed and conversa-
tional, the burgers are exceptional and the fresh exotic flowers add a final
*touché* (188/SUN BREAKFAST). Daily 12noon-11pm (Fri-Sat 12midnight). **CHP**

**83** **BAR BREL:** 342 4966. 39 Ashton Lane. Another Billy McAnnanie (Baby
*A1* Grand, Cottiers) translation of an idea from elsewhere. This is a Gallic
bar/bistro across the lane from the Cul de Sac (*see above*). Flagstone floor,
metal tables and enormous folding doors. No mistaking the Belgian influence in the cooking; fat, crispy chips served with large bowls of steaming
mussels, or with steak. No Belgian jokes, but Belgian beers and a good
wine list. Daily 11am-11pm (Fri-Sat till 12midnight). **INX**

**84** **UPSTAIRS AT THE CHIP:** 334 5007. 12 Ashton Lane. At other end of lane
*A1* from Cul de Sac (*see above*) and upstairs from The Ubiquitous Chip
(59/BEST RESTAUS), this is the wine bar and cheap seats version of the

celebrated restau. Some tables are around the gallery of the courtyard below. There's a different menu with some similar seafood and puds, as well as bar-type salads and soups, etc. The bill will be less and you still get the celebrated wine list. Lively atmos from the adj bar. LO 10.45pm. (189/SUN BREAKFAST)                                                                          **INX**

**85**  **TRON CAFÉ-BAR:** 552 8587. 63 Trongate. Attached to the important
*E4*  Tron Theatre (325/NIGHTLIFE), has undergone a major face-lift. The buzzing bar/bistro at the back has New Glas clientele, decent house wines and an eclectic  menu. Not always the best grub in the city, but definitely up there for atmos and generally good vibes. Bar food or restau. 7 days. LO 9-10.30pm depending on shows.                                                           **CHP**

**86**  **BOUZY ROUGE:** 221 8804. 111 W Regent St. Sister restau of the Bouzy
*C3*  Rouge in Airdrie (01236 763853) and now in Edin, this is an excellent unpretentious downtown bistro. Owned by the Brown family, it repeats the Airdrie formula of eclectic, affordable contemporary food and wine. Gr for breakfast and Sun lunch. 7 days, 9.30am-12midnight. Sun 12noon-12midnight. LO 10pm. Popular; booking may be necessary.                         **INX**

**FIREBIRD:** 1321 Argyle St. Report: 99/BEST PIZZA.

# THE BEST ITALIAN RESTAURANTS

**87** **√√√ SARTI:** 248 2228, 133 Wellington St, and 204 0440 (best number
*D3* for bookings), 121 Bath St. Glasgow's famed *emporio d'Italia* combining a deli in Wellington St, wine shop in Bath St and restaus in each. Gr bustling atmos. Cultivated and celebrated by anyone who has ever managed to get a table at lunchtime. Good pizza, specials change every day, *dolci* and *gelati* in super-calorific abundance. You may wait! LO 10.30pm. (101/PIZZAS) **CHP**

**88** **√ LA PARMIGIANA:** 334 0686. 447 Gr Western Rd. Sophisticated ris-
*B1* torante that blends trad service and contemporary Italian cuisine into a seamless performance. Carefully chosen dishes and wine list; solicitous service. Milano rather than Napoli. Expect to find Italians (who consider this to be one of the city's gr restaus – 62/BEST RESTAUS). Mon-Sat lunch and 6-11pm. Cl Sun. **MED**

**89** **√ LA FIORENTINA:** 420 1585. 2 Paisley Rd W. Not far from river and
*B4* motorway over Kingston Br, but app from Eglinton St (A77 Kilmarnock Rd). It's at the Y-jnct with Govan Rd. Trad tratt Little Tuscany (and pizzeria next door) in an imposing staid building with an angel on top. Always busy, usually seafood specials and off-hand waiters who break into the occasional aria. As Italian as you want it to be, gr atmos with enormous menu and wine list. Mon-Sat lunch and 5.30-11pm (though LO 9.30pm). Cl Sun. **MED**

**90** **EST EST EST:** 248 6262. 21–25 Bothwell St. Glas version of Edin George
*C3* St megarestau, as this UK chain expands into downtowns everywhere. Spacious, contemporary, stylish – pity, then, about the food. Service looks good, but may not deliver. Whatever – Blair New Britain loves this kind of dining out. 7 days. LO 10pm (10.45 w/ends). **INX**

**91** **RISTORANTE CAPRESE:** 332 3070. 217 Buchanan St. Basement café nr
*D3* the Concert Hall. Glaswegians (and footballers) love this place judging by the rogues' gallery of happy smiling punters. Checked tablecloths and crooning in the background create the authentic 'mamma mia' atmos. Friendly service, constantly mobbed (well, not *mobbed*). LO 10/11pm. Book at w/ends. **INX**

**92** **PAPERINO'S:** 332 3800. 283 Sauchiehall St. When you look into it, you
*C3* find good restaus of a certain type are often owned by the same people.

That explains why this ordinary-looking though smart restau is better than the rest – it's the Giovanazzi brothers who also own La Parmigiana (*see above*) and The Big Blue (235/PUB FOOD). Pasta and pizza here are always just fine. 7 days. LO 11pm/12midnight.                                  **INX**

**93**    **ANTIPASTI:** 337 2737. 337 Byres Rd. Popular restau on 2 levels that spills
*A1*    onto the st in warm weather, bringing a touch of *la dolce vita* to the corner of Observatory Rd. Good pasta. Breakfast time until late (12midnight w/ends). Also at 305 Sauchiehall St (332 9002). Same hours, food, and same vibe. 7 days. LO 10.30pm.                                  **INX**

**94**    **TREVI:** 334 3262. 526 Gr Western Rd. Tiny family-run tratt with celebrity
*B1*    photos next to cool football memorabilia on the walls. The staff can get a bit distracted on international fixture nights. Loyal clientele; specials change every day. Tasty home-made focaccia. Mon-Fri lunch and 6-10.30pm, Sat-Sun 6-10.30pm.                                  **INX**

**95**    **ARIGO:** 636 6616. 67 Kilmarnock Rd, Shawlands. Smart little Italian joint on
*xC5*    busiest stretch of this main drag. Waiters in the long aprons-u-like. Spare, colour-tint décor. Some surprises on the menu, e.g. *pollo e crozzo risotto* (with mussels). Proper wines. 7 days, lunch and dinner. LO 10.30pm.    **INX**

**96**    **FAZZI'S:** 332 0941. 67 Cambridge St. Across the rd from the Glas Thistle
*D3*    Hotel. This once gr deli/café (and some say it's gone rt down the pasta tube) included here more for nostalgia than now. Decent cappuccino. Mon-Sat 8am-10pm, Sun 11am-9pm.                                  **INX**

**97**    **LA SCARPETTA, BALLOCH:** 01389 758247. Balloch Rd nr the bridge.
*xB1*    Not perhaps many reasons to linger in Balloch – the loch (Lomond) here is not one of them, but this family-run restau is. Fave of writer A. L. Kennedy and she ain't easy to please. 7 days LO 10.30pm                **INX**

**ESCA:** 27 Chisholm St. Report: 78/BEST BISTROS.

**THE BIG BLUE:** 445 Gr Western Rd. Report: 235/PUB FOOD.

# THE BEST PIZZA

**98**
*D4, D3*  ✓ **PIZZA EXPRESS:** 221 3333. 151 Queen St and 402 Sauchiehall St (332 6965). The national chain who set the pizza standard here in 2 well-situated and classy restaus. Always a reliable standby when pizza's the only thing you can agree on and it's sometimes handy that you can't book.

**99**
*A3*  ✓ **FIREBIRD:** 334 0594. 1321 Argyle St. Big-windowed, spacious bistro at the far W end of Argyle St. Mixed modern menu but notable for wood-smoked dishes, of which their light, imaginative pizzas are excellent. 11am-12midnight (till 1am w/ends). **INX**

**100**
*A1*  **LITTLE ITALY:** 339 6287. 205 Byres Rd. Ready-made slices and 3 sizes of superb made-to-order takeaway pies. You'll have to wait, but it's worth it. Have a coffee. Mon-Thu 8am-10pm, Fri-Sat 8am-1am, Sun 5-10pm. (197/TAKEAWAY)

**101**
*D3*  **SARTI:** 248 2228. 133 Wellington St and 121 Bath St. Excellent, thin-crust pie, buffalo mozzarella and freshly-made *pomodoro*. 6 days, 8am-10pm. Cl Sun. Full report: 87/ITALIAN RESTAUS.

**102**
*B2*  **SAL E PEPE:** 341 0999. 18 Gibson St. Nr Glas Univ, this is the newest of the new crop of Tuscan-influenced Italian bistros and part of the Di Maggio family chain (175/KID-FRIENDLY). Good thin-crust base and a chilli *pomodoro* option that makes a change for veggies. 7 days, 9.30am-11pm.

**103**
*C3*  **CINE CITTÀ:** 332 6789. 327 Sauchiehall St. Trad oven-baked, thin-based pizza with all the usual freshly-prepared goodies that go on top; in the nite-zone. 7 days until 11pm.

**104**
*D3, C3*  **SANNINO:** 332 8025, 61 Bath St, and 332 3565, 61 Elmbank St. Famous for its enormous 16 inch pizzas, made for sharing. You can half and half the toppings. 7 days, 12noon-12midnight.

# THE BEST INDIAN RESTAURANTS

**105**
xC1

✔ **KILLERMONT POLO CLUB:** 946 5412. 2022 Maryhill Rd. The more genuine traditions of the days of the Raj are still in evidence at Killermont. Within a hill-top restau, at the Milngavie end of Maryhill Rd, you will find courteous manners, attentive service and a clubby atmos in the front rm, which is kept as a shrine to all things polo (and they *do* run their own team). The food is fresh and light, and the spices are sprinkled with care. Here Indian cuisine is taken seriously and they experiment – the introduction of their Dum Pukht menu (slow cooked) has been a huge success. Lunch seriously inx. Lunch (not Sun) and 5pm-12midnight (LO 10.30pm).  **MED**

**106**
B3

✔ **MOTHER INDIA:** 221 1663. 28 Westminster Terr. A kitchen-style restau where 'on-the-bone', a touchstone of authentic Indian home-cooking, is used to gr effect. Tired of the old trad buffet round, they've devised a new app where you can make up your own buffet – as many dishes as you like all freshly prepared. Lots of vegn choice. V relaxed neighbourhood atmos. BYOB. 7 days, lunch and LO 11pm, 11.30pm Fri/Sat.  **INX**

**107**
B3

✔ **CRÈME DE LA CRÈME:** 221 3222. 1071 Argyle St. The biggest, the most flash (and god knows they love flash) restau in town – or any-where for that matter – so *they* say. Still at the hot edge of all things cur-ried and they even show movies (*sic*), incl cartoons (177/KID-FRIENDLY). Frequently busy with office parties and leaving-dos, which keeps the place buzzing. Behind the flambé and the razzmatazz this is a restau that is run with care and, dare we say, precision. 7 days, lunch (not Sun) and LO 11pm.  **MED**

**108**
A1, B3

✔ **ASHOKA ASHTON LANE:** 357 5904. 19 Ashton Lane. Front-line curry shop for students from Glas Univ, just up the lane. V popular, v customer-led, so the food is strong on flavour and generously portioned. Can do no wrong, some say. **ASHOKA WEST END:** 339 0936. 1284 Argyle St. Has always been a good, simple and dependable place to go for curry, but now seeming pricey to the faithful. Still, the healthy option menu is a good idea and on Sun family night, kids eat free. Both 7 days, lunch and open till 12midnight (W End even later).  **INX**

**109**
B3

**MR SINGH'S INDIA:** 204 0186. 149 Elderslie St. In an area stuffed with curry houses, this one shows panache and some design. Menu is a tri-umph of trying to please. And they do. 7 days, lunch and LO 11.30pm.  **INX**

**110** **CAFÉ INDIA:** 248 4074. 171 N St. Enormous brasserie, big on a glamour
*B3* that seems a bit time-warped now, but the food is pretty good. The extensive menu is busy with herbs and spices and is not merely hot. A night on
the town kind of joint. Buffet and à la carte, Sun-Mon. 7 days, lunch and
LO 11.30pm/12midnight. **INX**

**111** **SHISH MAHAL:** 339 8256. 68 Park Rd. First-generation Indian restau that
*B2* still, after 30 yrs, remains one of Glasgow's faves. At last in '99 a major
refurb has brought it back into the light. Menu also completely recharged
and the toilets seriously posh. Many different influences in the cooking. 7
days. Till 11pm/12midnight. **INX**

**112** **KAMA SUTRA:** 332 0055. 331 Sauchiehall St. Part of the Ashoka group,
*C3* this restau has built a reputation for good food. An extensive and adven-
turous menu where each dish comes with a breakdown of contents and
region of origin. Extracts from the original Indian sex-guide dotted here
and there are peered at, surreptitiously, but décor seems a bit ragged
now. 7 days, lunch and till 12midnight (Fri-Sat till 1am). **INX**

**113** **THE ASHOKA:** 221 1761. 108 Elderslie St. Confusingly, no relation to
*B3* those above. Designery interior but that old pink pakora sauce still runs
through the veins. Once voted No. 1 in the 'Best curry houses in Scotland'
– that's a matter of taste but it is hot (and hot). Mon-Sat lunch, 7 days dinner. LO 11.30pm. **INX**

**114** **SHIMLA PINKS:** 423 4488. 777 Pollokshaws Rd. V serviceable Indian
*xC5* restau in Shawlands on the S side of town. Another branch in Johnstone
(01505 322588 at 4 William St) and part of a national chain hailing from
Brum. Only Indian restau in Glas recommended by Michelin. 7 days. Cl
lunch Sat/Sun. LO 11.30pm. **INX**

# THE BEST FAR-EASTERN RESTAURANTS

**115**
**B2**
✓ **THAI FOUNTAIN:** 332 2599. 2 Woodside Cres. Charing Cross, nr M8, Mitchell Library, etc. The best Thai in town (and probably in Scotland). Owned by Chinese Mr Chung (*see* Amber Regent, *below*), but the Thai chefs know a green curry from a red. Tom yam excellent and weeping tiger beef v popular with those who really just want a steak. Lots of prawn and fish dishes and real vegn choice. Lunch and LO 11pm. Cl Sun. **MED**

**116**
**A3**
✓ **THAI SIAM:** 229 1191. 1191 Argyle St (W End side). Trad homely (if crepuscular) atmos but fashionable clientele who swear it has the prawniest crackers and greenest curry in town. Prop/chef Pawina Kennedy ensures authenticity and a packed house at w/ends. Lunch Mon-Fri, LO 11pm. Cl Sun. **MED**

**117**
**A2**
✓ **FUSION:** 339 3666. 41 Byres Rd. Small, stylish and reasonably authentic Japanese bistro at bottom end of Byres Rd. Beef, chicken, salmon and vegn sushi/sashimi combos. Generally minimalist approach, incl wines and puds. Excellent value (how do they do it?). Lunch Tue-Sat, dinner Tue-Sun, 6pm-12midnight (but they may close earlier and the chefs do dictate). Same people opening (much larger) conveyor belt sushi bar in city centre, summer 2000. **CHP**

**118**
**E4**
✓ **MAO:** 564 5161. Corner of Brunswick and Wilson St in Merchant City. Bright, hip east-Asian restau transplanted not, of course, from Beijing but from Dublin. Good service, right-on wine-list. Open all day. 7 days. LO 10/11pm. **INX**

**119**
**D3**
✓ **AMBER REGENT:** 331 1655. 50 W Regent St. Elegant Cantonese restau that prides itself on courteous service and the quality of its food. The menu is trad with dishes designed to be eaten using chopsticks, although cutlery, of course, is provided. Candle-lit booths, sumptuous décor and a creditable wine list. Quite romantic, and just about always in *Michelin*. Lunch, LO 11pm (Fri 11.30pm, Sat 12midnight). Cl Sun. **MED**

**120**
**D4**
**HO WONG:** 221 3550. 82 York St, in city centre nr river, betw Clyde St and Argyle St. Discreet, urbane Pekingese/Cantonese restau which relies on its reputation and makes few compromises. Décor dated now, but still up-market clientele; roomful of suits at lunch and champagne list. Notable for seafood and duck. Good Szechuan. Lunch (not Sun) and LO 11.30pm. **MED**

**121** **PEKING INN:** 332 8971. 191 Hope St. The revolving hot-plate/server at
*D3* the centre of the table was an innovation when introduced here. Since
then there has been many a slip 'twixt cup and lip in the course of
lengthy, exploratory meals fuelled by endless hot saki. Famous for its
spicy, Szechuan specials; and good times. Lunch and LO 11.15pm (w/ends
12.15am). **MED**

**122** **LOON FUNG:** 332 1240. 417 Sauchiehall St. Poss Glasgow's most
*C3* 'respected' Cantonese restaus. Traditionally the place where the local
Chinese community meet for lunch with their families and on a
Sun/Mon/Tue, the pace is fast and friendly while the food, as you would
expect, is fresh and authentic. Everybody on chopsticks. 7 days, 12noon-
10/11pm. **MED**

**123** **THE NOODLE BAR:** 333 1883. 482 Sauchiehall St. Authentic, Chinese-
*C3* style noodle bar, 100m from Charing Cross. Along with **CANTON
EXPRESS** opp at 407 Sauchiehall St (332 0145), two gr fast-food joints
with genuine, made on the spot – in the wok – food late into the AM.
Quite groovy. 7days, 12noon-5am. (181/180/LATE-NIGHT RESTAUS) **CHP**

**124** **AMBER RESTAURANT:** 339 6121. 130 Byres Rd. Trad Chinese restau with
*A1* an informal attitude and helpful staff. Recently extended selection of
vegn dishes. V popular takeaway/home-delivery service; their chow mein
is the best in the W End. Lunch except Sat-Sun and 5-11.30pm. **INX**

**125** **CHINA TOWN:** 353 0037. 42 New City Rd. Out of centre and out of Glas;
*C2* in fact you're in Hong Kong (almost). Endless food for lunch (esp Sun) or
dinner. Divine dim sum. If you love Chinese food, you must come here. 7
days, 12noon-11.30pm. **INX**

**126** **ICHIBAN:** 204 4200. 50 Queen St. Upstairs noodle bar based loosely on
*D4* the Wagamama formula. Ramen, udon, soba noodle dishes; also chow
meins, tempuras and other Japanese snacks. Long tables, eat-as-it-comes
'methodology'. Light, calm, hip. Lunch and LO 11pm (10pm Sun). **INX**

# THE BEST MEXICAN RESTAURANTS

*Glas has innumerable restaus and café-bars with Mexican choices on a menu that mixes food from all over (best to stick to the potato skins). The places below are close to genuine Mex (UK style):*

**127**
**E4**
**PANCHO VILLAS:** 552 7737. 26 Bell St. Bright, colourful restau free of the cluttered cantina stereotype, run by real, live Mexican, Maira Nunez. Menu in Spanish/ingredients in English. No burritos ('an American invention'). Plenty of veggie choices but you really have to try the *albondigas en salsa* (that's spicy meatballs). Mon-Sat lunch and 6-11pm, Sun until 10pm. **INX**

**128**
**D4**
**CANTINA DEL REY:** 552 4044. 6 King's Court in E End nr St Enoch's glasshouse. Frozen margaritas a must in this spacious bar/restau which actually does feel like a cantina. Fajitas (with floury tortillas and spicy dips) a favourite among the *comidas* (which also includes blackened fish) and brought sizzling across the rm to your table. Free nachos; you keep on drinking. 7 days, 12noon till LO 10pm (Fri-Sat till 11pm). **INX**

**129**
**xA2**
**SALSA:** 337 1416. 184 Dumbarton Rd. Western off-shoot of the Cantina (*see above*), smaller, more neighbourhood-friendly. Spicy salsas of the title and all the things they accompany. As with all Mexican places, food can vary with the chef, most of whom have never been N, never mind S, of the Rio Grande, but here it's more conscientious than most. Good vegn choice. 7 days, 12noon-10pm (Fri 11pm). **INX**

**130**
**D3**
**TEX MEX:** 332 8338. 198 Bath St. Western extension of original in Edin and every bit as slammin'. More Tex than Mex, though chicken-fried steak notable by its absence, and howzabout some corn bread while we're at it. Adj Sublime Bar goes a bit Alamo at the w/end. 7 days, lunch and dinner. LO 10-11pm. **INX**

# THE BEST RESTAURANTS FROM AROUND THE WORLD

**131** ✓ **OBLOMOV:** 339 9177. 372 Gr Western Rd, nr Kelvinbridge.
*B1* Bar/restau with E European 'bohemian' twist. Small (12 tables) raised dining area with light and bar meals during day and heartier à la carte. Most dishes have Euro influence with some classics, e.g. blinis, goulash, strudel. Drink vodka. Often must book! Lunch and LO 8.30pm. Bar till 12midnight/1am. Gr Western Rd establishment now joined by a sister at 24 Candleriggs (552 4251). (232/PUB FOOD)                                    **INX**

**132** **CAFÉ SERGHEI:** 429 1547. 67 Br St, just over the Jamaica St (or Glas) Br.
*D4* Greek island evenings on a bleak rd heading S, a restau in an interesting conversion of a former bank with upstairs balcony beneath impressive cupola. In a tough world, this place has survived. Talkative waiters advise and dispense excellent Greek grub, incl vegn dishes. Fri is Greek dancing night. Lunch (not Sun) and 6-11pm, 7 days.                                    **INX**

**133** **PONTE VECCHIO:** 572 1881. 333 Gt Western Rd opp Oblomov (*see*
*B1* *above*) as it happens. Not a merely Italian restau as you might think from the title and most of the menu, but a Spanish-Italian joint with a genuine paella, risotto and a way with the *gambas*. Nice place too. 7 days, lunch and LO 10.15pm.                                    **INX**

**134** **STRAVAIGIN:** 334 2665. 28-30 Gibson St. The best fusion restau in town,
*B2* with influences from all over, though mainly E of Suez. Report: 52/BEST RESTAUS.

**135** **BAR BREL:** 342 4966. 39 Ashton Lane. Belgian would you believe?
*A1* Report: 83/BEST BISTROS.

**STRAVAIGIN** 'the best fusion restaurant in town, with influences from all over' (pages 29 and 45)

# THE BEST FRENCH RESTAURANTS

**136** **78 ST VINCENT:** 221 7710. 78 St Vincent St. Impressive split-level rm with
*D3* an enormously high ceiling and a big mural by Glas artist Donald
McLeod. Stylish cuisine balancing the tried and tested with some touch-
es of originality. Slightly formal with an atmos of discreet efficiency. Not
bad wines. Lunch (not Sun) and LO 10.30pm (10.45pm Sat-Sun).   **MED**

**137** **THE BRASSERIE:** 248 3801. 176 W Regent St. Related to Rogano (63/BEST
*C3* RESTAUS), so seafood is their forte and menu has seasonal v Scottish note.
Busy in evenings, but you can usually find a nook for that tête-à-tête. Here
you will find a genuine steak tartare. Good wine list, especially bin-ends
and halves. Mon-Fri 12noon-11pm, Sat lunch and 6-11pm. Sun, parties
only.   **MED**

**138** **FROGGIE'S:** 572 0007. 53 W Regent St. Café/bistro with French owners
*D3* and French home-cooking app. Gone a bit cajun/creole of late, but there
are still a few reminders left, viz the classic Marseillaise *soupe de poisson*.
Bustling brasserie atmos. Some reasonable wines and you can BYOB.
Open every day, best to book at w/ends. Mon-Sat 9am-12midnight; Sun
5pm-12midnight.   **INX**

**139** **PIERRE VICTOIRE:** 221 7565. 91 Miller St. A surviving Pierre from the
*D4* shakedown which followed Pierre Levicky's 'bankruptcy' and general
demise. Still a reasonable lunch and French bistro supper at v affordable
prices. Lunch and 5-10.30pm.   **INX**

**140** **CAFÉ DU SUD:** 332 2054. 8 Clarendon St. Popular intimate restau tucked
*C2* away behind St George's Cross. Mediterranean/French-style cooking
from husband-and-wife team who run it with an emphasis on the personal touch. Everything seems fresh and home-made. Better book. Tue-
Sat 12noon-3pm and 6-10.30pm. Cl Sun and Mon. Lunch Fri/Sat only, dinner Tue-Sat. LO 9.45pm.   **INX**

47

**141**
*A2*
✓✓ **TWO FAT LADIES:** 339 1944. 88 Dumbarton Rd. Informal and bright restau that serves some of Glasgow's most underrated food. Quality and freshness of seafood and imaginative cooking, in the hands of chef/proprietor Calum Mathieson. A reliably fine prospect whether you're a fishhead or not, and a bloody good place – no pun, no hype intended. Pre-theatre menu. Sensible short wine list. Mon/Tue-Sat 6-10pm, lunch Fri-Sat. (60/BEST RESTAUS)                              **MED**

**142**
*C3*
✓✓ **GAMBA:** 572 0899. 225a W George St, in basement at corner of W Campbell St. 1998 addition to the hitherto limited selection of seafood restaus in Glas and an instant catch. Mostly down to stylish setting and snappy service, as well as excellent fresh fish unfussily presented *à la mode*. Exemplary wine list. Unlike many, open on Mon (cl Sun). Lunch and dinner. LO 10.30pm but may stay open later so check. (51/BEST RESTAUS)                              **MED**

**143**
*xB1*
✓ **GINGERHILL:** 956 6515. Hillhead St, Milngavie. Upstairs at the end of the main st in this northern suburb of Glas (you are at the start of the W Highland Way), is a restau run entirely by women mostly from the island of Gigha (like much of the seafood they serve). Fixed menu and daily specials depending on what's landed. Vegn options and some char-grilled meat. One dinner sitting only, Thu-Sat (other nights if there are more than 6 of you); light lunches Mon-Sat. BYOB, no corkage.    **MED**

**ROGANO:** 11 Exchange Pl. Report: 63/BEST RESTAUS.

# THE BEST VEGETARIAN RESTAURANTS

**144**
**E4**   ✓ **THE 13TH NOTE:** 553 1638. 50-60 King St. Good attitude/good vibes café-bar with sometimes live music downstairs (Tue/Thu). Extended and big range menu from excellent vegeburgers (100% less meat than MacDonald's) to Indian and Greek dishes. All suitable for vegans. Organic booze on offer, but also normal Glas bevvy. 7 days, 12noon-12midnight. Food LO 10.30pm. Also 13th Note Club at Clyde St. (259/LIVE MUSIC)

**145**
**B2**   ✓ **GRASSROOTS:** 353 3278. 48 Woodlands Rd. The foremost emporium for all things organic in Glas. Now has a restau round the corner at 97 St Georges Rd (333 0534). This is proper food, prepared before your eyes. Round the world dishes as vegn food should be and some simply splendid salads. Calming as well as healthy. 7 days 10am-10pm. (185/SUN BREAKFAST) **CHP**

**146**
**B1**   **BAY TREE:** 334 5898. 403 Gr Western Rd. Long-established vegan restau nr Kelvinbridge. Wide range of dishes, esp Greek, Turkish and Arabic (owners are Iraqis). All strictly vegan, the sole concession being a jug of milk marked 'cows'. 7 days till 9pm (Sun till 8pm). (186/SUN BREAKFAST) **CHP**

**147**
**B1**   **CAFÉ ALBA:** 337 2282. 61 Otago St. Popular neighbourhood café with excellent, trad vegn food. Hot dishes of the day, good salads/dressings and home-made cakes, scones and slices. Hungry univ crowd, so there's not much left beyond 2.30pm. Mon-Sat 10am-5pm. (153/BEST TEAROOMS) **CHP**

**148**
**B3**   **THE ASHA:** 221 7144. Elderslie St. Intimate, vegn restau among many other Indians. All dishes can be made to order; your choice of sauce and chilli-ness. 3 fixed-price Thalis and a selection of starters that are moreish than most. Some wines, but a jug of lager is probably the answer here. Lunch (except Sun), and 5-11.30pm. **INX**

**THE GRANARY:** 82 Howard St, nr St Enoch Centre. Report: 152/BEST TEAROOMS.

*Restaus serving good vegn food but which are not exclusively vegn:*

**YES, PUPPET THEATRE, THE UBIQUITOUS CHIP** and **THAI FOUNTAIN:** Reports: 57/65/59/61/BEST RESTAUS.

**BABY GRAND, TRON CAFÉ-BAR, ARTHOUSE GRILL** and **GROUCHO ST JUDES:** Reports: 71/85/69/72/BEST BISTROS.

**MOTHER INDIA:** 28 Westminster Terr. Report: 106/INDIAN RESTAUS.

**CAFÉ GANDOLFI:** 64 Albion St. Report: 150/BEST TEAROOMS.

**SARTI** 'Glasgow's famed *emporio d'Italia*' (pages 38 and 51)

# THE BEST TEAROOMS AND COFFEE SHOPS

**149**
D3

✓ ✓ **SARTI:** 248 2228. 133 Wellington St and 121 Bath St. Full report: 87/ITALIAN RESTAUS, but mentioned here just in case you want a light snack or an excellent cappuccino – definitive. 8am-10pm.

**150**
E4

✓ ✓ **CAFÉ GANDOLFI:** 552 6813. 64 Albion St, Merchant City nr City Halls. The vaguely bohemian, Europe-somewhere atmos, the stained glass and the heavy, over-sized wooden furniture create a unique ambience that has stood the fashionability test of recent times. The food is light and imaginative and served all day. You may have to queue (because it's good). 7 days, 9am-11.30pm, Sun from 12noon. (184/SUN BREAKFAST)

**151**
A1

✓ ✓ **TINDERBOX:** 339 3108. 189 Byres Rd, on busy corner with Highburgh Rd. Stylish, designery but unlikely to date, a kind of state-of-the-art neighbourhood coffee shop. Stuff for kids, stuff to buy. Snacks and Elektra, the good-looking coffee machine. 7 days, 8am-10pm.

**152**
D4

✓ **THE GRANARY:** 226 3770. 82 Howard St, beside/behind the glass pyramid of the St Enoch Centre towards river. A calm style-free oasis away from the bustling shoppers on Argyle St that serves mainly vegn dishes but the emphasis is on home-baking. The apple pie is still the best in town. Hard to believe that this place exists in an area decimated by the mall-mongers. *Vive la resistance!* Mon-Sat 8.30am-6pm, Sun 11am-5pm.

**153**
B1

✓ **CAFÉ ALBA:** 61 Otago St. Just after the dog-leg on this busy st that's always in danger of falling into the river you'll find this supremely unruffled little café. Fresh mainly vegn fare, none of which exists much beyond lunchtime, and home-baked cakes that also have a tendency to disappear quickly. Draws a slightly arty (but not starving in garrets obviously) crowd. Mon-Sat 10am-5pm. (147/VEGN RESTAUS)

**154**
D4

✓ **MANGO AND STONE:** 221 3449. Princes Sq. Juice bar upstairs in Princes Sq at the top of the escalator. Mainly takeaway, but some seats on concourse. Excellent and healthy juice combos incl 'the Detox'. Also bagels, muffins, smoothies – the usual, but here done with some panache. Excellent coffee. 7 days till 6pm (Sun 5pm).

**155**
C3, D4

**THE WILLOW TEAROOMS:** 217 Sauchiehall St. Another level (The Gallery), has been added upstairs, and a new sister tearoom has now opened at 97 Buchanan St. Both, under the discerning eye of proprietor

Anne Mulhern, recreate the interiors of the original Miss Cranston's Tearooms, designed by C.R. Mackintosh. 30 blends of loose-leaf tea, all manner of cakes, scones and sandwiches and now, hold on … a wee glass of wine. Mon-Sat 9.30am-4.30pm. (315/MACKINTOSH)

**156**
*D3*
**CAFÉ ROBERTA:** 204 0860. 84 Gordon St, opp main canopied entrance to Central Stn. Popular downtown foodstop and famous cappuccino on your way to the train (or the work). 7 days. Mon-Sat 7.30am-7pm, Sun 10.30am-5pm.

**157**
*xA5*
**EXHIBITION CAFÉ:** 353 4779. 10 Dumbreck Rd, Bellahouston Park. On the ground floor of House for an Art Lover (317/MACKINTOSH). This bright rm has a modern Spanish feel; tan leather couches, tubular steel chairs and gallery space. Nicely prepared, light, lunch menu without fuss, like the surroundings. Excellent latte/espresso/cappuccino. Daily 10am-10pm (till 4pm Fri and Sun).

**158**
*C3*
**BRADFORDS:** 245 Sauchiehall St. Coffee shop/restau upstairs from the flagship shop of this local and estimable bakery chain. Familiar wifie waitresses, the macaroni cheese is close to mum's and the cakes and pies from downstairs represent Scottish bakery at its best. Mon-Sat 9am-5.30pm.

**159**
*D3*
**WESLEY OWENS, THE CHAPTERHOUSE:** 26 Bothwell St. A self-serve coffee shop at the back of a bookshop. Wholesome and home-baked; busy Christian rendezvous, behind the tracts and concordances. Mon-Sat 8.30am-4.30pm.

**160**
*D3*
**THE JENNY TRADITIONAL TEAROOMS:** 20 Royal Exchange Sq, opp new Gallery of Modern Art. Trad they are; inside, a chintzy parlour just as you might like to imagine it (though not perhaps off a main st in Glas). Sombrely lit and low-voiced for the serious business of taking tea (several varieties) with scones, cakes (not all home-made – tut-tut) and their famous fudge. Hot dishes and interesting sandwiches. Busy pavement tables in summer. 7 days, 8am-6.30pm (Sun till 6pm).

**161**
*xC5*
**TASHA BLANKITT:** 423 5172. 378 Cathcart Rd. An out-of-the-way and unusual gift/coffee shop/bistro S of the river with a loyal following. 'Hampstead in Govanhill' home-cooking that's truthful, often imaginative and selective; micro's only there to heat things up. Mon lunch only, Tue-Sat lunch and LO 8pm (Fri-Sat 12midnight), Sun 10.30am-6pm. Dinner w/ends only, 7-11pm. (171/KID-FRIENDLY)

**162** **LA FOCACCIA:** 337 1642. 291 Byres Rd. Italian coffee shop on busy Byres
*A1*  Rd with freshly-made sandwiches on a variety of continental breads, strong java and cakes and pastries. Those tiny wrought-iron and polished wood island thingies to perch at and babelicious counter staff – all gals … this is, after all, an Italian gaff. Soave's ice cream. Mon-Sat 7am-11pm, Sun 9am-10pm.

**163** **STARBUCKS:** 353 3149. 27 Sauchiehall St opp Concert Hall and branch-
*D3*  es (33 Bothwell St and 13 Renfield St). Formerly Seattle Coffee Company from NW USA at the forefront of the caffeine revolution. Excellent coffee, ambience and service. They practically invented the flavoured variants. 7 days till 7pm (8pm Thu).

**164** **COSTA COFFEE:** 221 9305. Royal Exchange Sq and innumerable branch-
*D3*  es incl Waterstones, Sauchiehall St. On a sunny day, you can't miss it – many tables o/side. The expanded version of the regular coffee house. All the steamy noises and aromas, double-filled sarnies, etc. plus flapjacks and some hot dishes, but coffee is their business. A swift espresso should see you round the Gallery of Modern Art (268/OTHER ATTRACTIONS).

# GREAT CAFÉS AND GREASY SPOONS

**165**
*A2*

✓ ✓ **UNIVERSITY CAFÉ:** 87 Byres Rd. When your granny, in the lines of the well-known song, was 'shoved aff a bus', this is where she was taken afterwards and given a wee cup of tea to steady her nerves. People have been coming here for generations to sit at the 'kneesy' tables and share the salt and vinegar. Run by the Verecchia family who administer advice, sympathy and pie, beans and chips with equal aplomb. A gem. Daily till 10pm (w/ends till 10.30pm). Cl Tue. Takeaway open later.

**166**
*xC5*

✓ ✓ **THE UNIQUE:** 223 Allison St. Not exactly central, but if you're on the S side you'll find the best fish 'n' chips in town here. Through the curtain in the café they serve lunches, fish teas and spam fritters. Veg oil used. Old-fashioned hrs, viz 8.15am-1.15pm, 3-8pm. That's right, 8pm – closed!

**167**
*A1*

✓ **GROSVENOR CAFÉ:** 35 Ashton Lane, behind Byres Rd nr Hillhead Stn. For over 30 yrs they've been serving hot, filled rolls and bowls of steaming broth to students, and all the rest of us who have happily crammed into the wee booths. New patio at rear and licence. More extensive suppery menu after 7pm. 7 days, 9am-11pm (Mon till 7pm, Sun till 5.30pm).

**168**
*xE4*

✓ **COIA'S CAFÉ:** 473 Duke St. Since 1928, supplying this E End high st with ice cream, gr deal breakfasts and the kind of comforting lunch (you would call it dinner) café-bar places just cannot do. There's a telly in the corner but it's really only there to spark off open debate. Sit-in or takeaway. Sweeties of all sorts; and Havana cigars. 7 days, 7.30am-9pm (LO 7.30pm); Sun from 11am.

**169**
*xC1*

**CAFÉ D'JACONELLI:** 570 Maryhill Rd nr the Queens Cross Church (310/MACKINTOSH). Neighbourhood caff with toasties, macaroni cheese and ice cream to go that's been here for ever. Disappearing Glasgow! Take to the baguettes. 7 days, 9am-10pm.

**170**
*xA5*

**ALLAN'S SNACK BAR:** 6 Storie St, Paisley. Off the High St, a chip shop with classic greasy spoon adj and a chips-with-everything menu in a Paisley days-gone-by atmos. Happy waitresses. Mon-Thu 11am-7pm, Fri-Sat 11am-8pm. Cl Sun.

**JACK MCPHEES:** 285 Byres Rd. Report: 176/KID-FRIENDLY.

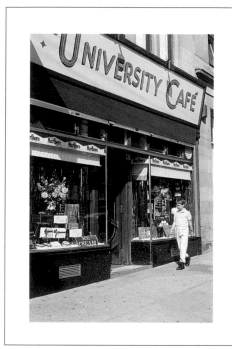

**UNIVERSITY CAFÉ** 'people have been coming here
for generations to sit at the "kneesy" tables' (page 54)

**171**
xC5

✓ **TASHA BLANKITT:** 423 5172. 378 Cathcart Rd. Bit out of the way, but not far from Pollokshaws Rd on the S side. A friendly spot to take the kids, commandeer a comfy corner and have some macaroni cheese. High chairs and half portions. 7 days, 8.30am-5.30pm (Sun 10.30am-4.30pm). (161/BEST TEAROOMS)

**172**
xC1

✓ **THE BLACK BULL HOTEL, KILLEARN:** 01360 550215. Take them for a run! Main sq in village on A81 towards Aberfoyle. Gr pub food (40/HOTELS O/SIDE GLAS), but esp if you've got kids and a fine day. Enclosed grd and adventure playground in parkland out the back, plus views of distant hills. Sound nice? You'd better believe it. 7 days.

**173**
D3

**TGI FRIDAYS:** 221 6996. 113 Buchanan St. The Glas branch of the national chain adored by kids because of the way they get fussed over and are given, pretty much, a free run of the place. The food is from everywhere via America and when added, free-hand, to the crayon drawings on the tablecloth, can quite spectacular. Huge range of cocktails available for parents who may need them. 7 days, 11am-11.30pm, Sun till 11pm.

**174**
B4

**HARRY RAMSDEN'S:** Paisley Rd W, beside M8 flyover – not far from centre, but difficult without a car. Not a bad branch of the national chain that caters well for kids. Greasy, cooked in lard and in cheerfully tacky surroundings, the chips and peas, sausage and fishcakes come in kids' portions and there's a playground to throw up into before you get back in the car.

**175**
A1
xC5
D4

**DI MAGGIO'S:** 334 8560. 61 Ruthven Lane, off Byres Rd, W End; 632 4194, 1038 Pollokshaws Rd, on a busy corner S of the river; and 248 2111, 21 Royal Exchange Sq. Bustling, friendly pizza joints with good Italian attitude to bairns. High chairs, special menu. 7 days.

**176**
A1

**JACK MCPHEES:** 285 Byres Rd. Squeaky booths, gingham table covers ... Cuthbert, Dibble and grub. Kids' meal and drink £1.95. Beat that you MacBurger Wimpy King Huts! 6 days, 8am-10pm, Sun till 7pm.

**177**
B3

**CRÈME DE LA CRÈME:** 221 3222. 1071 Argyle St. Big (huge), bustling Indian emporium which makes special allowances for kids (there are 40 high chairs available!), incl cartoons on giant screens. 7 days, lunch and LO 11.30pm. (107/INDIAN RESTAUS)

**178**
xE2

**FAMILY FUN PUB:** 0345 023028 (link-line). Belziehill 'Farm' off Jnct 5 of M74 on A725 to Coatbridge. It just sounds awful, but they have 'funday roasts', an ice-cream factory where you make your own and a Charlie Chalk menu for 'them'. But then kids are easy to please, no? Well, you will keep having them! 7 days.

# THE BEST LATE-NIGHT RESTAURANTS

**179**
**B2** ✓ **INSOMNIA/CRISPINS DELI:** 564 1700. 38 Woodlands Rd. 24hr café/deli that dispenses food, infusions, strong coffee and drinks to those who just *will not go to their beds*. In a rm full of higgledy-piggledy bits of furniture, baths full of goldfish and a clock noticeable by its absence, Glasgow's demi-monde plot and sip tea into the wee hrs of the afternoon. **7 days, 24hr.**

**180**
**C3** ✓ **CANTON EXPRESS:** 332 0145. 407 Sauchiehall St. The first fast-food Chinese joint on this block and still the genuine fast Chinese article. Not as wok-tastic as once was, but still feels like Hong Kong to us. 7 days, **12noon-4am.**

**181**
**C3** **THE NOODLE BAR:** 333 1883. 482 Sauchiehall St. Major competition to the above (even gets the edge in opening hrs). Authentic, Chinese fast food, no frills (ticket service and eezee-kleen tables). The noodle is 'king' here; cooking is taken seriously. 7 days, **12noon-4.30am.** (123/FAR-EASTERN RESTAUS)

**182**
**C3** **KING'S CAFÉ:** 332 0898. 71 Elmbank St. Here for yrs, for that special, deep-fried pizza need that sometimes, inexplicably, gets you at 3am. Not er … plush. Restau **till 11pm**; takeaway **till 5am Thu/Fri/Sat.**

**183**
**E4** **GUIDO'S CORONATION RESTAURANT:** 552 3994. 55 Gallowgate. Nr the Barrowland for as long as people have been going there. Fish and chips and home-made pizza/ice cream. Sit-in or takeaway. **Sun-Thu till 1am, Fri-Sat till 2am.**

*The following are also open till late 7 days:*

**CRÈME DE LA CRÈME:** 1071 Argyle St. Report: 107/INDIAN RESTAUS. **11pm.**

**BABY GRAND:** Elmbank Gdns, Charing X. Report: 71/BEST BISTROS). **12pm.**

**PIZZA EXPRESS:** Sauchiehall St/Queen St. Report: 98/PIZZA. **11.30pm.**

**ASHOKA ASHTON LANE:** Ashton Lane. Report: 108/INDIAN RESTAUS. **12.30am.**

**MR SINGH'S INDIA:** Elderslie St. Report: 109/INDIAN RESTAUS. **11.30pm.**

**LOON FUNG:** Sauchiehall St. Report: 122/FAR EASTERN RESTAUS. **11.30pm.**

**184**
**E4**

✓ **CAFÉ GANDOLFI:** 552 6813. 64 Albion St. Atmospheric rm, with soft daylight filtering through the stained glass and the comforting, over-sized wooden furniture. This is a pleasant start to another Sun, that day of rest and more shopping made even better with some baked eggs, a pot of tea and the Sun papers. **From 12noon**. (150/BEST TEAROOMS)

**185**
**B2**

**GRASSROOTS:** 97 St Georges Rd at Charing X. The proper healthy Sun start in calm rm a million miles from the motorway below. **Opens at 10am**. (145/VEGN RESTAUS)

**186**
**B1**

**BAY TREE:** 403 Gr Western Rd. This excellent caff (146/VEGN RESTAUS) pro-vides another antidote to the toxins of Sat night. A hearty vegan break-fast is served all day. **From 11am**.

**187**
**xA1**

**COTTIER'S:** 93 Hyndland St, off Hyndland Rd. Off the top of Hyndland St nr Highburgh Rd. Deep in the hefty-mortgage belt of Hyndland, this con-verted church probably gets more of a congregation now than it ever did. Eclectic menu from fruit plate to the full monty and eggs benedict to cajun kedgeree. Papers provided. **12noon-4pm**. (76/BEST BISTROS)

**188**
**A1**

**CUL DE SAC:** 44 Ashton Lane, off Byres Rd. Almost a tradition now, the smart relaxed place to phase into Sun. Clubby staff, so revival may take until late afternoon. The fry-up includes potato scones and comes in a vegn version, and there are the better-than-average burgers and exotic crêpes. Brunch **12.30pm-4pm**. (82/BEST BISTROS)

**189**
**A1**

**UPSTAIRS AT THE CHIP:** 334 5007. 12 Ashton Lane. 'Sair heid' or not, their Bloody Marys are the best in town and combined with a veggie breakfast (gr potato crowdie), famously restorative. Selection of papers. Unhurried. **From 12.30pm**. (84/BEST BISTROS)

**190**
**E4**

**BABBITY BOWSTER:** 552 5055. 16 Blackfriars St. The seminal Merchant City bar/hotel recommended for many things (237/PUB FOOD, 251/DRINK-ING OUTDOORS), but worth remembering as one of the best and earliest spots for Sun breakfast. **From 9am**.

# THE BEST TAKEAWAY PLACES

**191**
A1
**NAKED SOUP:** 334 6200. 106 Byres Rd. First of the new soup-to-go places that we might expect to take hold in Scotland. Perhaps not best location for office lunches, but otherwise absolutely the right idea. 8 fresh (organic where poss) soups daily and choice selection of smoothies. Sit-in or go. 7 days, 9am-6pm, Sun 12-5pm.

**192**
xC5
**MISE EN PLACE:** 424 4600. 122 Nithsdale Rd. S side specialist caterer and deli run by Suzanne Ritchie, who knows that rocket leaves are not enough. Everything from dinner *à deux* to full-on alfresco bash with cool waiters and other trimmings. Delivered to your door or drop in for delish lunch. New caff next door from late '99. Mon-Fri 9.15am-5.45pm, Sat 9.15am-2pm.

**193**
D4, D3
**O'BRIENS (IRISH SANDWICH BARS):** 221 2239 (Central Stn). 4 branches at time of going to press of the Irish version (a tad more opportunistic than ours) of a modern coffee/sandwich/muffin place. In busy places like Argyle St, Sauchiehall St, St Enochs and Central Stn. 7 days till 5pm (stn till 9pm).

**194**
D3
**HUNGRYS:** 353 1889. 98 Bath St. 'American-style' deli/sandwich shop in downtown Glas. It's a long way from 34th St, NYC, but it's much better than most on these blocks, as long lunch queues attest. Several kinds of bread, good soup. Try a pepper and tuna mayo on herb focaccia. Mon-Fri 8am-4pm.

**195**
D3
**FIRST CHOICE:** 331 2272. 138 Renfield St. At the top of the town, across the st from Scottish Television. Good selection of cheeses and sandwich meats – their pastrami and Swiss toastie is v popular and v Glas. Freshly-made coffee and a selection of cakes – but the empire biscuits don't last much beyond 11am. What is it about STV and empires? Mon-Fri 6.30am-5pm, Sat 6.30am-3pm.

**196**
D3, C3
**NUMBER ONE SANDWICH ST:** 248 2050, 104 St Vincent St and 221 2002, 9 Waterloo St. 2 other downtown locations where office-workers and shop assistants descend in droves for assembly-line and some bespoke sandwiches and baked potatoes. Betw them they produce over 1,000 lunches a day. Mon-Fri 8am-4pm.

**197**
A1
**LITTLE ITALY:** 339 6287. 205 Byres Rd. Gr pizza focaccia and pasta, fresh-ly-baked breads, ice cream, loadsa Italian wines and a no-bad (meaning 'not at all bad') cup of coffee. Mon-Thu 8am-10pm, Fri-Sat 8am-1am, Sun 5-10pm. (100/PIZZA)

**198**
xB1
**TOSCANA:** 956 4020. 46 Station Rd, Milngavie. It's a long way from town, but this family-run Italian café does gr takeaway pasta and pizza and home-made puds. Till 10pm.

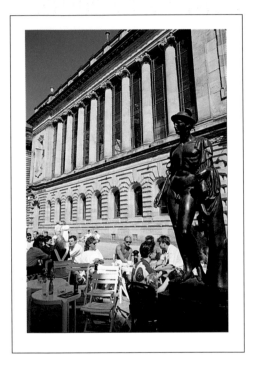

Alfresco dining at the Italian Centre in the Merchant City

# WHERE TO DRINK

# SOME GREAT 'GLASGOW' PUBS

*Pubs you won't find anywhere else; uniquely Glas.*

**199**
**B2**
✓ **THE HALT BAR:** 160 Woodlands Rd. On the old tram route W, this Edwardian pub remains largely unspoilt. Original counter and snug intact, but v much moves with the times. Always gr atmos – model of how a pub should look and feel. Live music and DJs some nights. (211/'UNSPOILT' PUBS, 257/LIVE MUSIC) Open till 11pm (12midnight w/ends).

**200**
**D4**
✓ **CORINTHIAN:** 191 Ingram St. Mega makeover of impressive listed building to form cavernous bar/restau, 2 comfy lounge/cocktail bars and a superb restau (49/BEST RESTAUS) nr George Sq and Gallery of Modern Art. Awesome ceiling in main rm much much better than megabars elsewhere. Food in main rm excellent and good coffee. Older, richer, well-heeled clientele, some Armani. Totally Glas. 7 days, till 12midnight. (Piano bar Thu-Sun.)

**201**
**D3**
✓ **THE HORSESHOE:** 17 Drury St. A mighty pub since 1884 (and before) in the small st betw Mitchell and Renfrew Sts nr Central Stn. Early example of this style of pub, dubbed 'gin palaces'. Island rather than horseshoe bar and an upstairs lounge where they serve high tea. The food is amazing value (231/PUB FOOD). Caledonian and Maclays. Daily till 12midnight.

**202**
**D4**
✓ **VICTORIA BAR:** 157 Bridgegate. 'The Vicky' is in the 'Briggait', one of Glasgow's oldest streets, nr the Victoria Br over the Clyde. Once a pub for the fishmarket and open odd hrs, now it's a howf for all those who like an atmos that's old, friendly and uncontrived. Real ales. Mon-Sat till 12midnight, Sun till 11pm. (337/NIGHTLIFE)

**203**
**D4**
✓ **SCOTIA BAR:** 112 Stockwell St. Nr the Victoria (*see above*), late-1920s Tudor-style pub with a low-beamed ceiling and intimate, woody 'snug'. Long the haunt of folk musicians, writers and raconteurs. Music and poetry sessions, folk and blues. Daily till 12midnight. (336/NIGHTLIFE)

**204**
**D4**
✓ **CLUTHA VAULTS:** 167 Stockwell St. This and the pubs above are part of the same family of trad Glas pubs. The Clutha (ancient name for the Clyde) has a Victorian-style interior and an even longer history. Known for live music. Mon-Sat till 12midnight, Sun till 11pm. (334/NIGHTLIFE)

**205**
**E4**
✓ **BLACKFRIARS:** 36 Bell St. Contemporary, but pub-like in middle of Merchant City – predates most of those around it. Huge selection of European and E European beers. Eclectic menu (238/PUB FOOD) till 6pm. Regular programme of live music. 7 days 12noon-12midnight.

**206**
**B2**
✓ **UISGE BEATHA:** 246 Woodlands Rd. 'Oo-i-skay Bay' (or something like that) means 'the water of life' and is a unique Highland outpost in the city. Shooting-lodge chic wearing a bit thin now, but cosy. More than a mere draught of the Gael. Good grub at lunchtime. Related to one of the gr Highland bars, The Drover's Inn, Inverarnan. Sun-Thu till 11pm, Fri-Sat till 12midnight.

**207**
**D3**
**BAR 10:** 10 Mitchell Lane, off Buchanan St. Opp new Lighthouse and nr the Tunnel, this is a well-placed 'cool' bar. Mongrel furniture and sliced-brawn tiles, high ceiling and design by Ben Kelly of Manchester's Hacienda fame, this place looks like it's been transported from Canal St, NYC. Good food, gossip and strong coffee served with a shot of iced water during the day; the place to go pre-club at night. Regular DJs at w/ends. (240/THESE ARE HIP)

**208**
**B3**
**MCPHABBS:** 23 Sandyford Pl. 2 blocks W of Charing Cross. Non-aligned boozer, more of a 'shebeen' than anything else. *Laissez-faire* attitude. Postage-stamp patio at rear, tasty bar food, endorsed by local MP George Galloway. Good malts. 7 days, till 12midnight Fri-Sat. (234/PUB FOOD)

**209**
**xA2**
**LISMORE:** 206 Dumbarton Rd, main rd W after Byres rd. Lismore/Liosmor named after the long island off Oban. Gr neighbourhood (Partick) bar that welcomes all sorts. Gives good atmos, succour and malts. Daily till 12midnight.

**210**
**E4**
**THE MITRE:** 12 Brunswick St, but more in the lane behind Trongate opp the backwards EMPIRE sign by Douglas Gordon who may be inside. Despite many fashionable bars nearby in the Merchant City, this more trad pub is where the not dressed up people drink. Cheap food, karaoke upstairs on a Sat night. V old labour. Till 11pm, 12midnight w/ends. (215/'UNSPOILT' PUBS)

*One type of bar/café/restau that Glas does v well is the Style-bar, with complete makeover à la mode. For a limited lifespan they are the place to be seen. At time of going to press the best of these are:*

**AIRORGANIC** (56/BEST RESTAUS), **GROUCHO ST JUDES** (12/LESS EXP HOTELS), **BAR CE LONA** 427 Sauchiehall St, and **ARTHOUSE** (2/BEST HOTELS).

WEST END

GREAT WESTERN ROAD

BYRES ROAD

Kelvingrove Park

Charing Cross

SAUCHIEHALL STREET

River Clyde

SECC

River Clyde

Kingston Bridge

SOUTH SIDE

River Clyde

• 206
• 199

• 208

← 209

207 •
207 •

201 •

200 •

210 •

205 •
205 •

203 •
204 •• 202

Glasgow Green

POLLOKSHIELDS

*Of course it's not necessarily the case that when a pub's done up it's spoilt, or that all old pubs are worth preserving, but some have resisted change and that's part of their appeal. The following places don't have to recreate 'atmos'. Most of them close no later than 12midnight.*

**211**
**B2**
✓ **THE HALT BAR:** 160 Woodlands Rd. In the classic trad of the stand-up bar with a 'snug' (for the ladies), behind a wooden partition, with 'pulpit' serving-hatch. Varied (free) live music through the back (257/LIVE MUSIC). Sun-Thu till 11pm, Fri-Sat till 12midnight. Music usually from 9pm. (199/GR GLAS PUBS)

**212**
**C3**
✓ **THE GRIFFIN (AND THE GRIFFINY AND THE GRIFFINETTE):** 266 Bath St. Corner of Elmbank St nr King's Theatre. Built 1903 to anticipate the completion of the theatre and offer the patrons a pre-show pie and a pint. Stand at the Edwardian Bar like generations of Glaswegians. Main bar still retains 'snug' with a posh, etched-glass partition; booths have been added but the atmos is still 'Old Glasgow'. Sun-Thu till 11pm, Fri-Sat till 12midnight. (230/PUB FOOD)

**213**
**xE2**
**THE ROWAN TREE, UDDINGSTON:** 12km SE of centre via M74. In Old Mill Rd off Main St where sign points (in opp direction) for Bothwell Castle (379/O/SIDE GLAS). A cottagey pub in the shadow of the world-famous Tunnock's Caramel Wafers factory and long frequented by the wafermakers. Food at lunchtime, coal fire in winter, folk music on Fri. Maclays. Mon-Sat till 11.45pm, Sun till 11pm.

**214**
**E4**
**THE SARACEN'S HEAD:** Gallowgate, nr Barrowlands. An establishment of this name has existed in the neighbourhood since 1755, playing host to a multitude of colourful characters; not least Boswell and Johnson, on the return leg of their grand Highland tour. This, the most recent incarnation, opened in 1905 and is famous for its lethal 'White Tornado' cider. The atmos is more 'wild west' than E End, although the 'one singer, one song' rule still prevails. 7 days. Cl 10.30pm during week.

**215**
**E4**
**THE MITRE:** The lane of Brunswick St, off Argyle St opp C&A. Untouched by the 'gentryfiers' and full of character. Gem of a bar, just quietly getting on with its business. Bit of music at w/ends, food at lunch, Belhaven; nothing fancy. 7 days till 11pm or 12midnight. (210/GR GLAS PUBS)

**216**
**xC5**
**M J HERAGHTY:** 708 Pollokshaws Rd. More than a touch of the Irish about this pub and easily more authentic than recent imports. A local with loyal regulars who'll make you welcome; old pub practices still hold in this howf in the sowff. Sun-Thu till 11pm, Fri-Sat till 12midnight.

**217** **BRECHIN'S:** 803 Govan Rd. Nr jnct with Paisley Rd W and motorway
*A5* over-pass. Established in 1798 and, as they say, always in the same family.
A former shipyard pub which, despite the proximity to Rangers FC, is not
partisan. It's behind the statue of shipbuilder Sir William Pearce (which,
covered in sooty grime, was known as the 'Black Man') and there's a feline
'rat-catcher' on the roof (making it a listed building). Unaffected neighbourhood atmos. Mon-Sat till 11pm, Sun till 6.30pm.

**218** **THE OLD TOLL BAR:** 1 Paisley Rd W. Opp the site of the original
*B4* Parkhouse Toll, where monies were collected for use of the 'turnpikes'
betw Glas and Greenock. Opened in 1874, the original interior is still
intact; the *fin de siècle* painted glass and magnificent old gantry preserved under order. A 'palace pub' classic. Real ale and some single malts.
7 days till 11pm.

**219** **THE HORSESHOE:** 17 Drury St. The celebrated city-centre bar with the
*D3* famous 'longest bar in the world' and an assortment of Old and New
Glaswegians ranged along it. (201/GR GLAS PUBS, 231/PUB FOOD)

**220** **BAIRDS BAR and THE DISTRICT:** 2 bars from opp sides of the gr divide.
*E4* **BAIRDS** in the Gallowgate adj Barrowlands is a Catholic stronghold
*xA5* green to the gills where, on days when Celtic play at home up the rd at
Parkhead, you'd have to be in by 11am to get a drink. **THE DISTRICT,** 252
Paisley Rd W, Govan, nr Ibrox Park, is where Rangers supporters gather
and rule in their own blue heaven. Both pubs give an extraordinary
insight into what makes the Glas time bomb tick. Provided you aren't
wearing the wrong colours (or say something daft), you'll be very welcome in either.

# THE BEST REAL-ALE PUBS

*Pubs on other pages may purvey real ale, but the following are the ones where they take it seriously and/or have a good choice.*

**221**
**B3**
✓ **BON ACCORD:** 153 N St. On a slip rd of the motorway swathe nr the Mitchell Library. One of the first real-ale pubs in Glas. Over 100 malts as well as up to 12 beers; always McEwan's 80/-, Theakston and Old Peculier, plus many guest ales on hand pump. Food at lunchtime and light bites till 9pm. Light, easy-going atmos here, but they do take their ale seriously; there's even a 'tour' of the cellars if you want it. Mon-Sat till 12midnight, Sun till 11pm.

**222**
**A2**
✓ **THREE JUDGES:** 141 Dumbarton Rd, opp the bottom of Byres Rd. Named after the triumvirate of boxing judges that used to own it. These days you're more likely to find professors than practitioners of the 'gentlemanly art'. Maclays and 9 guest ales that change regularly from a cast of hundreds. 7 days.

**223**
**A1**
**TENNENTS:** 191 Byres Rd. Nr the always-red traffic lights at Univ Ave, a big, booming watering-hole of a place where you're never far away from the horseshoe bar and its several excellent hand-pumped ales, incl Maclays, Caledonian and Theakston. Revamped to take it into the next century, but the 'old century' crowd will still be there.

**224**
**E4**
**BABBITY BOWSTER:** 16 Blackfriars St. In a pedestrianized part of the Merchant City and just off the High St, a highly successful pub/restau/hotel (20/LESS EXP HOTELS); but the pub comes first. Maclays is heavily featured and make their own Babbity Thistle Ale, but there's always an English guest and lots of malts. Food all day (237/PUB FOOD), occasional folk music (esp Sun), o/side patio (251/DRINK OUTDOORS) and exhibs. Proprietor Fraser Laurie has thought of everything.

**225**
**D3**
**THE CASK AND STILL:** 154 Hope St. 8 ales (always Youngers No. 3, McEwan's 80/- and Old Peculier), but also noted for a mind-boggling range of malts. They've got over 200. Mon-Sat till 11pm/12midnight. Cl Sun.

**226**
**A2**
**THE BREWERY TAP:** 1055 Sauchiehall St, up W by the park nr the Univ. All-round studenty kind of bar with food all day till 9pm, music on Sat (jazz-blues) and at least 5 ales on tap. 7 days.

**227**
**xC5**
**THE TAVERNA:** 778 Pollokshaws Rd. Intimate wine bar/lounge on the S side with 2 Czech beers on draft and a large selection of German wheat-beers.

**228** **THE HORSESHOE:** 17 Drury St. Gr for lots of reasons (201/GR GLAS PUBS),
*D3* not the least of which is its range of beers: Caledonian, Greenmantle, Maclays and Bass on hand pump.

**229** **VICTORIA BAR:** 157 Bridgegate. Another pub mentioned before (202/GR
*D4* GLAS PUBS) where IPA, Maclays and others can be drunk in a dark woody atmos enlivened by occasional trad music (337/NIGHTLIFE).

# PUBS WITH GOOD FOOD

**230**
C3

✓ ✓ **THE GRIFFIN:** 266 Bath St. On corner of Elmbank St across from King's Theatre. The Griffin, the Griffiny and the Griffinette: they're always there on that corner and your basic pie/chips/beans *and a pint* will not be bettered at this price (£2.80 lunchtime, Griffin only at time of going to press, the equivalent 80 yrs ago of 8 old pence). Other staples available and a more elaborate menu in the lounge or the Griffinette next door. Food: 12noon-3pm and evenings till 7.30pm. Pub till 12midnight. (212/'UNSPOILT' PUBS)

**231**
D3

✓ ✓ **THE HORSESHOE:** 17 Drury St. The classic pub to be recommended for all kinds of reasons. But lunch is a particularly good deal with 3 courses for £2.60 (pie and beans still 80p), and old favourites on the menu like mushy peas, macaroni cheese, jelly and fruit. Lunch 12noon-2.30pm and all afternoon upstairs, incl high tea till 7.30pm (not quite the same atmos, but pure Glas). Pub open daily till 12midnight. (201/GR GLAS PUBS)

**232**
B1

✓ **OBLOMOV:** 339 9177. 372 Gr Western Rd, Kelvinbridge. Cool W End bar by Ron McCulloch (designer/entrepreneur of this parish). This time the timeless appeal of sepia, softly-lit pre-war kinda thing. Booths and chaises, big drapes. Crepuscular dining-rm. Contemporary menu. Their food is good and not too foreign. (131/AROUND THE WORLD). 7 days. Served 11.30am-8.30pm.

**233**
A3

✓ **AIRORGANIC:** 564 5200. 36 Kelvingrove St nr the park. Restau upstairs was definitely flavour of the month (or season 98/99), but snackier food in bar, e.g. Thai curry sandwiches, sushi boxes, so the hip place to graze. Open fire among cool minimalism and cool music. 7 days, 11am–11pm. (56/BEST RESTAUS)

**234**
B3

✓ **MCPHABBS:** 221 0770. 23 Sandyford Pl. 2 blocks W of Charing Cross. Gr Scottish/Irish bar food; smoked haddies, salmon and steaks, beef and Guinness stew, etc. Given the 'parliamentary seal of approval' by local MP George Galloway who particularly rates the stew. 7 days, open till 12midnight at w/ends. (208/GR GLAS PUBS)

**235**
B1

**THE BIG BLUE:** 445 Gr Western Rd. A modern bar/bistro in a gr uptown location literally on the (river) Kelvinside. Drinking may drown the eating later on, but till mid/late-evening there's excellent Italian pasta/pizza pub grub. LO 10/10.30pm. Bar till 12midnight.

**236** **THE DRUM AND MONKEY:** 93 St Vincent St, on corner of Renfield St.
D3 Cavernous but comfortable, and once fashionable bar/bistro with a sombre gentlemen's club atmos – 'the odd libation for the overworked'. Comfort and more contemporary food with a bistro through the back which has an à la carte menu in the evening. 7 days till 11pm.

**237** **BABBITY BOWSTER:** 16 Blackfriars St. Already listed as a pub for real ale
E4 and as a hotel (there are rms upstairs), the food is mentioned mainly for its Scottishness (haggis and stovies) and all-day availability. It's also pleasant to eat o/side on the patio/grd in summer. There is a restau upstairs (lunch Mon–Fri, dinner Mon–Sat) but we prefer down. Also breakfast served from 8am (Sun 9am). (224/REAL-ALE PUBS, 20/LESS EXP HOTELS)

**238** **BLACKFRIARS:** 36 Bell St. Candleriggs is one of the focal points in the
E4 Merchant City. Gr Glas pub for all-round ambience, provision of real ale and music, and food available all day till 12midnight (but drinkers loud after 9pm). (205/GR GLAS PUBS, 255/LIVE MUSIC)

**239** **FOX AND HOUNDS, HOUSTON:** On B790 village main st in
xA5 Renfrewshire, 30km W of centre by M8 jnct 29 (A726), then cross back under motorway on B790. Village pub with real fire and dining-rm upstairs for family meals and suppers. Folk come from miles around. Sun roasts. Lunch and 6-10pm (all day w/ends).

**STRAVAIGIN:** 28-30 Gibson St. Excellent pub food upstairs from one of the best restaus in town. Report: 52/BEST RESTAUS.

# THESE ARE HIP

**240**
*D4*
**BAR 10:** 221 8353. 10 Mitchell Lane, halfway up Buchanan St pedestrian precinct on the left. There's an NYC look about this joint that is so loved by its habitués, they make an exhib out of themselves. Designed by Ben Kelly of Hacienda fame, it has stood the fashion test and is as happening as ever. Good pre-club spot. The new **BLUE** across the way may fan the pre-club party. (207/GR GLAS PUBS)

**241**
*E4*
**BARGO:** 553 4771. 80 Albion St. In the Merchant City, this spacious, designer-theque is much in demand for fashion shoots and, of course, high-glam posing on a Sat night. Can be attractively, if not spookily, quiet during the week when surprisingly OK food is served.

**242**
*A1*
**CUL DE SAC:** 649 4717. 44 Ashton Lane. This upstairs bar is a perennial W End fave. Close to the underground for that last-minute dash into town to beat club curfews. (32/BEST BISTROS, 188/SUN BREAKFAST)

**243**
*D3, A2*
**BUDDA:** 221 5660. 142 St Vincent St. **LIVING ROOM:** 339 8511. 5 Byres Rd, nr bottom end. 2 perennially hip bars which kick in, esp Fri-Sat pre-club. This groove a turn-of-the-century thing. Will it last, now we've turned? Till 12midnight.

**244**
*D3*
**SPY BAR:** 221 7711. 151–155 Bath St. Central bar-restau kind of place though *The Herald* trashed the food bigtime not long after it opened (bit-of-everything menu from Cajun to pasta). Otherwise a funky basement bar where styly people gather. 7 days, 11am-12midnight (Sun from 6pm).

**245**
*D4*
**POLO LOUNGE:** 553 1221. 84 Wilson St. Urbane and stylish bar/disco by the irrepressible Stephen King. Unmistakably gay in the heart of the emerging quarter. Clubbable rather than clubby crowd until late on arranged around the comfortable furniture. Mellow Sun afternoons; papers and jazz. (345/GAY GLAS)

**246**
*D4*
**YANG:** 248 8484. 31 Queen St. Neon-lit style bar for trendy young things. Next door to Archaos (356/BEST CLUBS). May seem clinical/spartan for some tastes; it's the antithesis of the old Glas pub. (357/BEST CLUBS)

**AIRORGANIC:** 36 Kelvingrove St. Report: 233/PUB FOOD.

# THE BEST PLACES TO DRINK OUTDOORS

**247**
**xB1**
**LOCK 27:** 1100 Crow Rd. At the very N end of Crow Rd beyond Anniesland, an unusual boozer for Glas: a canalside pub on a lock of the Forth and Clyde Canal (276/WALKS IN THE CITY), a touch English (a v wee touch), where of a summer's day you can sit o/side. Excellent bar food, always busy. 7 days.

**248**
**A1**
**COTTIER'S:** 357 5825. 93 Hyndland St. First on the left after the swing park on Highburgh Rd (going W) and the converted church is on your rt, around the corner. Gr place for many reasons (76/BEST BISTROS, 187/SUN BREAKFAST), but a cold beer on a hot day sitting in leafy shade is one of the best; or into the evening – life can be good! 7 days.

**249**
**xA2**
**WICKETS HOTEL:** 334 9334. 52 Fortrose St. Probably best app via Dumbarton Rd, turning up Peel St before railway br. O/looking W of Scotland Cricket Ground (hence name). Large terr beer grd, made for long summer afternoons. You can at least imagine the thwack of balls in the distance. Good place to bring kids, even if you don't see them very often (Dad!). 7 days. (21/LESS EXP HOTELS)

**250**
**A1**
**ASHTON LANE:** As soon as the sun comes out, so do the punters. With the **CUL DE SAC** and **BAR BREL** at one end and **JINTY MCGINTY'S** at the other, benches suddenly appear and the whole lane becomes a cobbled, alfresco pub. It's the nearest Glas gets to Euro, even Dublin, drinking. 7 days.

**251**
**E4**
**BABBITY BOWSTER:** 552 5055. 16 Blackfriars St. Unique in the Merchant City for several reasons (224/REAL-ALE PUBS, 237/PUB FOOD), but in summer certainly for its napkin of grd in an area bereft of greenery. Though enclosed by surrounding sts, it's an oasis many head for. Feels like Soho, Soho NYC. Naw, feels like Glas. Always good crack. 7 days.

# GOOD LIVE MUSIC

*Many other places have live music but programmes and policies can vary quickly. Best to look out for posters or consult* The List *magazine, on sale fortnightly at all good newsagents.*

**252**
*C3* ✓ **KING TUT'S WAH WAH HUT:** 221 5279. 272 St Vincent St. Every bit as good as its namesake in Alphabet City used to be; the room for interesting new bands, make-or-break atmos and cramped. Bands on the club circuit play to a damp and appreciative crowd. See flyers. Doors open 8.30pm. Tickets at bar or Tower Records, Argyle St.

**253**
*C3* **NICE 'N' SLEAZY:** 333 9637. 421 Sauchiehall St at the W End. Not esp sleazy and fairly rock 'n' roll. Popular art school hang-out. Every flavour of alco-pop and voddie to drink. Good indie jukebox and Playstation for hire. Bands downstairs (esp Thu-Sun) with a nominal entrance charge. Usually from 9pm. All over before 12 midnight.

**254**
*D4, C3* **THE CATHOUSE:** 248 6606. 15 Union St, and **THE GARAGE**, Sauchiehall St, W End (same owners). Live rock clubs with mixed programme on various nights depending on availability of touring bands (other 'clubs' on other nights). Recent broadening of musical taste so no longer necessary to turn up with leather strides and pointy boots. Tickets in advance, as for King Tut's (*see above*).

**256**
*E4* **BLACKFRIARS:** 552 5924. 36 Bell St. Merchant City pub with everything (205/GR GLAS PUBS) which includes all kinds of live music and, if you are a player, 'Glasgow songwriters' on Tue nights features an open mic guest policy. Turn up early to book your spot. Free. (238/PUB FOOD)

**257**
*D4* **SCOTIA BAR and THE CLUTHA VAULTS:** 552 8681/552 7520. Nr each other in the E End nr the river and under same management (112 and 167 Stockwell St). Integral part of the Glas folk scene for yrs (334/336/FOLK MUSIC), but also readings and other sessions (e.g. Clutha has bluegrass and country). Glas Folk Club on Wed at Scotia and always at w/ends. Free. (203/204/GR GLAS PUBS)

**258**
*B2* **THE HALT BAR:** 564 1527. 160 Woodlands Rd. Gr pub rock atmos with booked live acts on Thu and 'open mic' spots on Wed and Sat. Music starts around 9pm and admn is free. (199/GR GLAS PUBS, 211/'UNSPOILT' PUBS)

**259**
*xA1* **COTTIER'S:** 357 5825. 93 Hyndland St. In the densely populated quadrant betw Dumbarton Rd and Byres Rd. A neighbourhood atmos to this converted church (not in, but off the top of Hyndland St nr Highburgh Rd); it has the same management as the Baby Grand (71/BEST BISTROS) and

Cathedral House (13/LESS EXP HOTELS). Restau upstairs (76/BEST BISTROS). Bar and theatre, on the ground level, serve as a platform for local talent and cult-ish acts from abroad. Regularly features special gigs with 3 or more bands on the bill and, occasionally, entire, musically-themed, w/ends. Expect good programming.

**260**
*D4*
**THE 13TH NOTE:** 221 0414. Café, 60 King St and Club, Clyde St. The vegn restau in King St (144/VEGN RESTAUS) and the gig thing down nr the river. Various combos of the indie or merely hip in both. These are the ones to watch. Tue-Sun 8pm-3.30am.

**ROGANO** 'an institution in Glasgow since the 1930s' (page 31)

**MUSEUM OF TRANSPORT** 'one of Scotland's most
fascinating museums' (page 82)

# WHERE TO GO IN TOWN

**KELVINGROVE ART GALLERY AND MUSEUM** 'huge Victorian sandstone edifice with awesome atrium' (page 79)

**260**
*A2*
✓ ✓ **KELVINGROVE ART GALLERY AND MUSEUM:** 287 2700. At westerly extension of Argyle St and Sauchiehall St by Kelvingrove Park. Huge Victorian sandstone edifice with awesome atrium. On the ground floor is a natural history/Scottish history museum. The upper salons contain the city's superb British and European art collection. There are strong contemporary exhibs as well as the permanent collection. Pipe-organ recitals every alternate Sun. Tearoom. The Museum of Transport (266/OTHER ATTRACTIONS) is across the rd. Mon-Sat 10am-5pm, Sun from 11am. **FREE**

**261**
*xC5*
✓ ✓ **THE BURRELL COLLECTION and POLLOK PARK:** 649 7151. S of river via A77 Kilmarnock Rd (over Jamaica St Br) about 5km, following signs from Pollokshaws Rd. Set in rural parkland, this hugely successful attraction is an award-winning modern gallery built to house the eclectic acquisitions of Sir William Burrell. Showing a preference for medieval works, among the 8,500 items the magpie magnate donated to the city in 1944 are artefacts from the Roman Empire to Rodin. The building itself integrates old doorways and whole rms reconstructed from Hutton Castle. Self-serve café and restau on the ground floor. **POLLOK HOUSE** and Grds further into the park (with works by Goya, El Greco and William Blake) is worth a detour and has, below stairs, the better tearoom. Both open Mon-Sat 10am-5pm, Sun from 11am. (277/WALKS IN THE CITY)
**BURRELL COLLECTION FREE/POLLOK HOUSE ADMN**

**262**
*xE3*
✓ **GLASGOW CATHEDRAL/PROVAND'S LORDSHIP:** 552 8198/552 8819. High St. Across the rd from one another they represent what remains of the oldest part of the city, which (as can be seen in the People's Palace, *see below*) was, in the early 18th century, merely a ribbon of streets from here to the river. The present Cathedral, though established by St Mungo in AD 543, dates from the 12th century and is a fine example of the v real, if gloomy, Gothic. The house, built in 1471, is a museum which strives to convey a sense of medieval life. Watch you don't get run over when you re-emerge into the 20th century and try to cross the st. In the background, the Necropolis piled on the hill invites inspection and offers a viewpoint and the full Gothic perspective. Mon-Fri 9.30am-4pm (not 1-2pm), Sun 2-4pm.

**263**
*xE5*
✓ **THE PEOPLE'S PALACE:** 554 0223. Reopened after renovations in spring 1998. App via the Tron and London Rd, then turn rt into Glas Green. This has long been a folk museum *par excellence* wherein, since 1898, the history, folklore and artefacts of a proud city have been

gathered, cherished and displayed. But this is much more than a mere museum; it is the heart and soul of the city and together with the Winter Grds adj, shouldn't be missed if you want to know what Glasgow's about. Tearoom in the Tropics, among the palms and ferns of the Winter Grds, will still be part of the attraction for any visitor in the future. Opening times as other museums (*see above*).                    **FREE**

**264**  **ST MUNGO MUSEUM OF RELIGIOUS LIFE AND ART:** 553 2557. In the
*xE3*  Cathedral precinct or sq dubbed 'Ft Weetabix' by Glas cabbies. Opened with some gnashing of teeth and wringing of hands in 1993, it houses art and artefacts representing the world's 6 major religions arranged tactfully in an attractive stone building with a Zen grd in the courtyard. The dramatic Dalì *Crucifixion* seems somehow lost, and the assemblage seems like a good and worthwhile vision not quite realized. But if you like your spirituality shuffled but not stirred, this is for you. The punters' comments board is always … enlightening. Mon-Sat 10-5pm, Sun from 11am.   **FREE**

**265**  **HUNTERIAN MUSEUM AND GALLERY:** 330 5431. Univ Ave. On one
*A1*  side of the st, Glasgow's oldest museum with geological, archaeological and social history displayed in a venerable building. The cloisters outside and the **UNIVERSITY CHAPEL** should not be missed. Across the st, a modern block contains part of Glasgow's exceptional civic collection – Rembrandt to the Colourists and the Glas Boys, as well as one of the most complete collections of any artist's work and personal effects to be found anywhere, viz that of Whistler. It's fascinating stuff, even if you're not a fan. There's also a print gallery and the superb **MACKINTOSH HOUSE** (311/MACKINTOSH). Mon-Sat 9.30am-5pm.                    **FREE**

1   2   3   4   5

A   B   C   D   E

M8

262

• 262

4

GALLOWGATE

• 263

5

Glasgow Green

HIGH STREET

DUKE ST

SALTMARKET

MERCHANT CITY

TRONGATE

Albert Bridge

Victoria Bridge

BALLATER STREET

GORBALS STREET

SOUTH SIDE

River Clyde

St ENOCH SHOPPING CENTRE

CITY OF GLASGOW

BUCHANAN BUS STATION

QUEEN STREET STATION

GEORGE SQUARE

Buchanan Galleries

SAUCHIEHALL STREET

CENTRAL STATION

BROOMIELAW

261 →

George V Bridge

Glasgow Bridge

Kingston Bridge

M8

GARSCUBE ROAD

GREAT WESTERN ROAD

WOODLANDS ROAD

BERKELEY STREET

SAUCHIEHALL STREET

ARGYLE STREET

Charing Cross

Kelvingrove Park

THE RIVER

BYRES ROAD

WEST END

• 265

• 260

DUMBARTON RD

CLYDESIDE EXPRESSWAY

River Clyde

SECC

Bells Bridge

PAISLEY ROAD WEST

POLLOKSHIELDS

# THE OTHER ATTRACTIONS

**266**
*A2*

**MUSEUM OF TRANSPORT:** 287 2700. Off Argyle St behind the Kelvin Hall and opp Art Gallery. May not seem your ticket to ride, but this is one of Scotland's most fascinating museums. Has something for everybody, esp kids. The reconstruction of a cobbled Glas st c1938 is an inspired evocation. There are trains, trams and unique collections of cars, motorbikes and bicycles. And model ships in the Clyde rm, in remembrance of a mighty river. Make a donation and the Mini splits in two. Mon-Sat 10am-5pm, Sun 11am-5pm. **FREE**

**267**
*xB1*

**BOTANIC GARDENS and KIBBLE PALACE:** 334 2422. Gr Western Rd. Smallish park close to R Kelvin with riverside walks (275/WALKS IN THE CITY), and pretty much the 'dear green place'. Kibble Palace (built 1873) is the distinctive domed glasshouse with statues set among lush ferns and shrubbery from around the (mostly temperate) world. A wonderful place to muse and wander. Grds open till dusk; palace 10am-4.45pm.

**268**
*D4*

**GALLERY OF MODERN ART:** 331 1854. Queen St. Central, controversial and housed in former Stirling Library, Glasgow's big visual arts attraction opened in a hail of art world bickering in 1996. Director Julian Spalding's choice of inclusion raised to record levels both the ire of critics and the interest of the public. This 'Modern Art' incl contemporary and populist from elsewhere, but little from the influential movements and bugger all from the Saatchi side in which many Glas artists have made notable contributions. Smart café up top. Same hrs as Museum of Transport (*see above*). **FREE**

**269**
*xE4*

**THE BARROWS:** (pronounced 'Barras') The sprawling st and indoor market area in the E End of the city around the Gallowgate. An experience, an institution, a slice of pure Glas. If you're only in town for one w/end, it's a must, and like no other market anywhere. Sat and Sun only.

**270**
*C2*

**THE TENEMENT HOUSE:** 333 0183. 145 Buccleuch St. Nr Charing Cross but can app from nr the end of Sauchiehall St and over the hill. The typical 'respectable' Glas tenement kept under a bell-jar since Our Agnes moved out in 1965. She had lived there with her mother since 1911 and wasn't one for new-fangled things. It's a touch claustrophobic, with hordes of visitors, and is distinctly voyeuristic, but, well … your house would be interesting, too, in 50 yrs time if the clock were stopped. Daily Mar-Oct 2-5pm. **ADMN**

**271**    **SHARMANKA KINETIC GALLERY:** 552 7080. 2nd floor, 14 King St,
*E4*    Trongate. A small and intimate experience compared with most of the
others on this page, but an extraordinary one. The gallery/theatre of
Russian emigre Eduard Bersudsky shows his meticulous and amazing
mechanical sculptures. He and his partner prod around to get them in
motion. Sat-Sun 12noon-4pm.

**272**    **GREENBANK GARDENS:** 10km SW of centre via Kilmarnock Rd,
*xC5*    Eastwood Toll, Clarkston Toll and Mearns Rd, then signposted (3km). A
spacious oasis in the suburbs; formal grds and 'working' walled grd,
parterre and woodland walks around elegant Georgian house. V Scottish.
Grds open AYR dawn-dusk, shop/tearoom Apr-Oct 11am-5pm.    **NTS**

**273**    **CITY CHAMBERS:** 287 2000. George Sq. The hugely impressive building
*D3*    along the whole E end of Glasgow's municipal central sq. Let's face it, it's
not often that one could seriously recommend a visit to the City Council
offices, but this is a wonderfully over-the-top monument to the days
when Glas was the second city of the empire, a cross between an Italian
Renaissance palace and an Escher marble maze. Guided tours Mon-Fri,
10.30am and 2.30pm.

**274**    **FINLAYSTONE ESTATE:** 01475 540505. 30km W of city centre via fast
*xA5*    M8/A8, signed off dual carriageway just before Pt Glas. Delightful grds
and woods around mansion house with many pottering places and
longer trails (and ranger service). Various 'attractions', e.g. that rare thing:
a walled grd and Victorian laundry and kitchen, etc. Visitor centre and
conservatory tearoom. Much better family outing than McDonalds or the
grd centre. 7 days, 10.30am-5pm.

**PAISLEY ABBEY:** 15km from Glas. Report: 284/BEST VIEWS, 378/O/SIDE
GLAS.

**BOTHWELL CASTLE, UDDINGSTON:** 15km E, via M74. Report:
379/O/SIDE GLAS.

*See page 9 for walk codes.*

**275** **KELVIN WALKWAY:** A path along the banks of Glasgow's other river, the
B2 Kelvin, which enters the Clyde unobtrusively at Yorkhill but first meanders
through some of the most interesting parts and parks of the NW city.
Walk starts at Kelvingrove Park through the Univ and Hillhead district
under Kelvin Br and on to the celebrated Botanic Grds (267/OTHER ATTRAC-
TIONS). The trail then goes N, under the Forth and Clyde Canal (*see below*)
to the Arcadian fields of Dawsholm Park (5km), Killermont (posh golf
course) and Kirkintilloch (13km from start). Since the river and the canal
shadow each other for much of their routes, it's possible, with a map, to
go out by one waterway and return by the other (e.g. start at Gr Western
Rd, return Maryhill Rd).

**START:** Usual start at the Eildon St (off Woodlands Rd) gate of
Kelvingrove Park or Kelvin Br. St parking only. **2-13+KM XCIRC BIKE 1-A-1**

**276** **FORTH AND CLYDE CANAL TOWPATH:** The canal, opened in 1790 and
D2 once a major short cut for fishing boats and trade betw Europe and
xC1 America, provides a fascinating look round the back of the city from a
pathway that stretches on a spur from Pt Dundas just N of the M8 to the
main canal at the end of Lochburn Rd off Maryhill Rd and then E all the
way to Kirkintilloch and Falkirk, and W through Maryhill and Drumchapel
to Bowling and the Clyde (60km). Much of the route is through the for-
saken or redeveloped industrial heart of the city, past waste ground,
warehouses and high flats, but there are open stretches and curious cor-
ners and, by Bishopbriggs, it's a rural waterway. More info from British
Waterways (332 6936). Revitalizing the whole Edin–Glas link is a major
Millennium project.

**START:** (1) Top of Firhill Rd (gr view of city from Ruchill Park, 100m further
on – 281/BEST VIEWS). (2) Lochburn Rd (*see above*) at the confluence from
which to go E or W to the Clyde. (3) Top of Crow Rd, Anniesland where
there is a canalside pub, Lock 27 (247/DRINK OUTDOORS), with tables o/side,
real ale and food (12noon-7/8pm). (4) Bishopbriggs Sports Centre,
Balmuildy Rd. From here it is 6km to Maryhill and 1km in the other direction to the 'country churchyard' of Cadder or 5km to Kirkintilloch. All
starts have some parking. **ANY KM XCIRC BIKE 1-A-1**

**277** **POLLOK COUNTRY PARK:** The park that (apart from the area around
xC5 the gallery and the house – 261/MAIN ATTRACTIONS) most feels like a
real country park. Numerous trails through woods and meadows. The

leisurely Sun guided walks with the park rangers can be educative and more fun than you would think (632 9299). Burrell Collection and Pollok House and Grds are obvious highlights. There's an 'old-fashioned' tea-room in the basement of the latter. Enter by Haggs Rd or by Haggs Castle Golf Course. By car you are directed to the entry rd off Pollokshaws Rd and then to the car park in front of the Burrell. Train to Shawlands or Pollokshaws W from Glas Central Stn.

**278** **MUGDOCK COUNTRY PARK:** 956 6100. Not perhaps within the city, but
*xB1* one of the nearest and easiest escapes. Park which incl Mugdock Moor, Mugdock Woods (SSSI) and 2 castles is NW of Milngavie. Regular train from Central Stn takes 20 min, then follow route of W Highland Way for 4km across Drumclog Moor to S edge of park. Or take Mugdock Bank bus from stn (not Sat) to end. By car to Milngavie by A81 from Maryhill Rd and left after Black Bull Hotel (on left) and before railway stn (over to rt) up Ellengowan Rd. Continue past reservoir then pick up signs for park. 3 car parks, visitor centre is at second one. Many trails marked out and further afield rambles. This is a godsend betw Glas and the Highland hills.

**5-20KM CAN BE CIRC BIKE 1-A-2**

**CATHKIN BRAES:** On S edge of city with impressive views. Report: 279/BEST VIEWS.

# THE BEST VIEWS OF THE CITY AND BEYOND

*Refer to Around Glasgow map on pages 116–17.*

**279**
**D3**
**CATHKIN BRAES, QUEEN MARY'S SEAT:** The southern ridge of the city on the B759 from Carmunnock to Cambuslang, about 12km from centre. Go S of river by Albert Br to Aikenhead Rd which continues S as Carmunnock Rd. Follow to Carmunnock, a delightfully rural village, and pick up the Cathkin Rd. 2km along on the rt is the Cathkin Braes Golf Club and 100m further on the left is the park. Marvellous views to N of the Campsies, Kilpatrick Hills, Ben Lomond and as far as Ben Ledi. Walks on the Braes on both sides of the rd.

**280**
**D3**
**QUEEN'S VIEW, AUCHINEDEN:** Not so much a view of the city, more a perspective on Glasgow's Highland hinterland, this short walk and sweeping vista to the N has been a Glaswegian pilgrimage for generations. On A809 N from Bearsden about 8km after last r/bout and 2km after the Carbeth Inn which is a v decent pub to repair to. Busy car park attests to its popularity. The walk, along path cut into ridgeside, takes 40-50 min to cairn, from which you can see The Cobbler (392/O/SIDE GLAS), that other Glas favourite, Ben Ledi and sometimes as far as Ben Chonzie 50km away. The fine views of L Lomond are what Queen Victoria came for. Further on is The Whangie (368/WALKS O/SIDE CITY). **1-A-1**

**281**
**D3**
**RUCHILL PARK:** An unlikely but splendid panorama from this over-looked, but well-kept park to the N of the city nr the infamous Possilpark housing estate. Go to top of Firhill Rd (past Partick Thistle football ground) over Forth and Clyde Canal (276/WALKS IN THE CITY) off Garscube Rd where it becomes Maryhill Rd. Best view is from around the flagpole; the whole city among its surrounding hills, from the Campsies to Gleniffer and Cathkin Braes (*see above*), becomes clear.

**282**
**D3**
**BAR HILL, TWECHAR, nr KIRKINTILLOCH:** 22km N of city, taking A803 Kirkintilloch t/off from M8, then the 'low' rd to Kilsyth, the B8023, bearing left at the 'black-and-white br'. Next to Twechar Quarry Inn, a path is signed for Bar Hill and the Antonine Wall. Steepish climb for 2km, ignore strange dome of grass. Over to left in copse of trees are the remains of one of the forts on the wall which was built across Scotland in the 2nd century AD. Ground plan explained on a board. This is a special place with strong history vibes and airy views over the plain to the city which came a long time after. **1-A-2**

**283** **BLACKHILL, nr LESMAHAGOW:** 28km S of city. Another marvellous
E4  outlook, but in the opp direction from above. Take jnct 10/11 on M74,
then off the B7078 signed Lanark, take the B7018. 4km along past
Clarkston Farm, head uphill for 1km and park by Water Board mound.
Walk uphill through fields to rt for about 1km. Unprepossessing hill which
unexpectedly reveals a vast vista of most of E central Scotland.     **1-A-2**

**284** **PAISLEY ABBEY:** About one Sat a month betw May and Oct (1-5pm) on
D3  Abbey 'open days', the tower of this amazing edifice can be climbed. The
tower (restored 1926) is 50m high and from the top there's a grand view
of the Clyde. Obviously this is a rare experience, but phone TO (889 0711)
for details; next Sat could be your lucky day. M8 to Paisley; frequent trains
from Central Stn.

**285** **LYLE HILL, GOUROCK:** Via M8 W to Greenock, then round the coast to
C3  relatively genteel old resort of Gourock where the 'Free French' worked in
the yards during the war. A monument has been erected to their memo-
ry on the top of Lyle Hill above the town, from where you get one of the
most dramatic views of the gr crossroads of the Clyde (Holy L, Gare L and
L Long). Best vantage-point is further along the rd on other side by trig pt.
Follow British Rail stn signs, then Lyle Hill. There's another gr view of the
Clyde further down the water at **HAYLIE, LARGS**, the hill 3km from town
reached via the A760 rd to Kilbirnie and Paisley. The island of Cumbrae
lies in the sound and the sunset.

**CAMPSIE FELLS and GLENIFFER BRAES**: 364/365/WALKS O/SIDE THE
CITY.

## SWIMMING AND INDOOR SPORTS CENTRES

*The best 2 pools, Arlington Baths (332 6021) and the Western Baths (339 1127), are private. Temporary memberships may be negotiable. Others are:*

**286**
*xE4*
**WHITEHILL POOL:** 551 9969. Onslow Dr parallel to Duke St at Meadowpark St in the E End nr Alexandra Park (phone for times but usually Mon-Fri till 8.30pm and Sat-Sun till 1.45pm). 25m pool with sauna/multigym (Universal).

**287**
*B2*
**NORTH WOODSIDE LEISURE CENTRE:** 332 8102. Braid Sq. Not far from St George's Cross nr Charing Cross at the bottom of Gr Western Rd. In a rebuilt area; follow AA signs. Modern pool (25m) and sauna/steam/sun centre. Mon-Fri 8/9am-7/8pm (Sat-Sun 10am-4pm).

**288**
*xC5*
**POLLOK LEISURE CENTRE:** 881 3313. Cowglen Rd. Not a do-your-lengths kind of a pool – more a family water outing. Mon-Fri 9.30am-9pm, Sat/Sun 10am-4pm.

**289**
*xA5*
**GOUROCK BATHING POOL:** 01475 631561. On rd S, an open-air heated pool on the Clyde. Gr prospect for summers like they used to be. (401/O/SIDE GLAS)

**290**
*A2*
**KELVIN HALL:** 357 2525. Argyle St by Kelvingrove Art Gallery and Museum (260/MAIN ATTRACTIONS). Major venue for international indoor sports competitions, but open otherwise for weights/badminton/tennis/athletics. Book hr-long sessions. No squash.

**291**
*xA2*
**SCOTSTOUN LEISURE CENTRE:** 959 4000. Danes Dr. Huge state-of-the-art sports multiplex. 10-lane pool, indoor halls and outdoor pitches. 9am-10pm, w/ends till 6pm.

**292**
*xE4*
**MARCO'S:** 554 7184. Templeton Business Centre (beside the fabulous Templeton Carpet Factory, by Glas Green in the E End). Like the Edin one, a labyrinthine and massively successful complex with squash/snooker/gym (Universal and First Class)/indoor jogging track (even though it is next to the Green). Nonmembers OK. 10am-10pm (Sat till 8pm). No pool.

**293**
*xC1*
**ALLANDER SPORTS CENTRE:** 942 2233. Milngavie Rd, Bearsden, 16km N of centre via Maryhill Rd. Best by car. Squash (2 courts) badminton/snooker and swimming pool (open late, but times vary; usually till 10.30pm Tue/Thu/Fri and 9pm Sat-Sun). Waiting list for gym.

## GOLF COURSES

*Glas has a vast number of parks and golf courses. The following clubs are the best open to nonmembers. Refer to Around Glasgow map on pages 116–17.*

**294**
**D3**
**CATHKIN BRAES:** 634 0650. Cathkin Rd, SE via Aikenhead Rd/Carmunnock Rd to Carmunnock village, then 3km. Best by car. Civilized hilltop course on the v southern edge of the city. Nonmembers Mon-Fri (though probably not Fri am).

**295**
**D3**
**HAGGS CASTLE:** 427 1157. Dumbreck Rd nr jnct 22 of the M8; go straight on to clubhouse at first r/bout. Part of the grounds of Pollok Park; a convenient course, perhaps overplayed, but not difficult to get on.

**296**
**D3**
**POLLOK GOLF CLUB:** 632 1080. On the other side of the White Cart Water from Pollok House and rather more up-market. Well-wooded parkland course, flat and well kept, but not cheap. Women not permitted to play.

**297**
**C3**
**GLEDDOCH, LANGBANK:** 01475 540711. Excellent 18-hole course adj and part of Gleddoch House Hotel (38/HOTELS O/SIDE GLAS). Restricted play.

## TENNIS

**298**
**B2,**
**xC5,**
**xA3**
Public courts (Apr-Sep), membership not required: **KELVINGROVE PARK** 6 courts, **QUEEN'S PARK** 6 courts, **VICTORIA PARK** 6 courts. Courts open 12noon-8pm.

## RIDING

**299**
**xC5**
**HAZELDEN, NEWTON MEARNS RIDING SCHOOL:** 639 3011. A77, 15km SW of city centre.

**300**
**xE2**
**KENMURE RIDING SCHOOL AND LIVERY YARD:** 772 3041. Kenmure Ave, Bishopbriggs, off A803 Kirkintilloch rd. Check opening times.

**TEMPLETON'S CARPET FACTORY** on Glasgow Green. Where one can truly state, 'They don't build them like that anymore'

*Apart from those listed previously (*MAIN ATTRACTIONS, OTHER ATTRACTIONS*) the following galleries are always worth looking into. The* Glasgow Gallery Guide, *free from any of them, lists all the current exhibs.*

**301**
**E4**
✓ ✓ **GLASGOW PRINT STUDIOS:** 552 0704. 22 King St. Influential and accessible upstairs gallery with print work on view and for sale from many of Scotland's leading and rising artists. Cl Sun. Print Shop over rd.

**302**
**E4**
✓ ✓ **TRANSMISSION GALLERY:** 552 4813. 28 King St. Cutting edge and often off-the-wall work from contemporary Scottish and international artists. Reflects Glasgow's increasing importance as a hot spot of conceptual art. Stuff you might disagree with. Cl Sun-Mon.

**303**
**C4**
✓ ✓ **MODERN INSTITUTE:** 248 3711. Robertson St. Not really a gallery – more a concept. Will Bradley's cutting-edge art ideas and occasional events. Sometimes exhibs, incl Glasgow Art Fair (*see below*).

**304**
**D3**
✓ ✓ **THE GLASGOW ART FAIR:** George Sq in tented pavilions. Held every yr in mid-Apr. Most of the galleries on this page and many more are represented; highly selective and good fun.

**305**
**C3**
✓ **COMPASS GALLERY:** 221 6370. 178 W Regent St. Glasgow's oldest established commercial contemporary art gallery. Their 'New Generation' exhib in Jul-Aug shows work from new graduates of the art colleges and has heralded many a career. Combine with the other Gerber gallery (*see below*). Cl Sun.

**306**
**C3**
✓ **CYRIL GERBER FINE ART:** 221 3095. 148 W Regent St. British paintings and esp the Scottish Colourists and 'name' contemporaries. Gerber, the Compass (*see above*) and Art Exposure (*see below*) have Christmas exhibs where small, accessible paintings can be bought for reasonable prices. Cyril will know what's good for you. Cl Sun.

**307**
**E4**
**ART EXPOSURE GALLERY:** 552 7779. 19 Parnie St. Behind the Tron Theatre. Showcase gallery with a friendly, down-to-earth attitude exhibiting the work of contemporary/graduate Scottish artists. Sort of 'affordable'. 11am-6pm. Cl Sun.

**308**
**E4**
**SHARMANKA KINETIC GALLERY:** 552 7080. 14 King St, nr Trongate. Upstairs. Extraordinary gallery (theatre?) full of the fully-working mechanical sculptures. W/ends 2-4pm. (271/OTHER ATTRACTIONS)

**GLASGOW SCHOOL OF ART** 'Mackintosh's supreme architectural triumph' (page 93)

*The gr Scottish architect and designer Charles Rennie Mackintosh (1868–1928) had an extraordinary influence on contemporary design. Glas is the best place to see his work.*

**309**
*C3*
✓ ✓ ✓ **GLASGOW SCHOOL OF ART:** 353 4500. 167 Renfrew St. Mackintosh's supreme architectural triumph. It's enough almost to admire it from the st (and maybe best, since this is v much a working college) but there are guided tours at 11am and 2pm (Sat 10.30am) of the sombre yet light interior, the halls and library. You might wonder if the building itself could be partly responsible for its remarkable output of acclaimed painters. The Tenement House (270/OTHER ATTRACTIONS) is nearby.

**310**
*xC1*
✓ ✓ **QUEEN'S CROSS CHURCH:** 870 Garscube Rd, where it becomes Maryhill Rd (corner of Springbank St). Built 1896-99. Calm and simple, the antithesis of Victorian Gothic. If all churches had been built like this, we'd go more often. The HQ of the Charles Rennie Mackintosh Society, which was founded in 1973 (phone 946 6600). Mon-Fri 10am-5pm, Sat 10am-2pm, Sun 2-5pm. **DONATION**

**311**
*A1*
✓ ✓ **MACKINTOSH HOUSE:** 330 5431. Univ Ave. Opp and part of the Hunterian Museum (265/MAIN ATTRACTIONS) within the univ campus. The Master's house has been transplanted and methodically reconstructed from the next st (they say even the light is the same). If you've ever wondered what the fuss is about, go and see how innovative and complete an artist, designer and architect he was, in this inspiring yet habitable set of rms. Mon-Sat 9.30am-5pm (cl 12.30-1.30pm). Cl Sun.

**FREE**

**312**
*B5*
✓ ✓ **SCOTLAND STREET SCHOOL:** 429 1202. 225 Scotland St. Opp Shields Rd underground and best app by car from Eglinton St (A77 Kilmarnock Rd over Jamaica St Br). Entire school (from 1906) preserved as museum of education through Victorian/Edwardian and wartimes. Original, exquisite Mackintosh features, esp tiling and powerfully redolent of happy school days. This is a uniquely evocative time capsule. Café and temporary exhibs. Mon-Sat 10am-5pm, Sun 11am-5pm. **FREE**

**313**
*D4*
✓ **THE LIGHTHOUSE:** 221 6362. Mitchell Lane, off Buchanan St by Warner Bros store. Glasgow's legacy from its yr as UK City of Architecture and Design. Changing exhibs in Mackintosh's 1893–5 building for *The Glasgow Herald* newspaper. Also houses an interpretation

centre on the gr architect with fantastic rooftop views from the corner tower, plus **BLUE** (75/BEST BISTROS) and **THE DOOCOT**.

**314**
xA3 ✓ **THE HILL HOUSE, HELENSBURGH:** 01436 673900. Upper Colquhoun St. Take Sinclair St off Princes St (at Romanesque tower and TO) and go 2km uphill, taking left into Kennedy Dr and follow signs. A complete house incorporating Mackintosh's typical total unity of design, built for Walter Blackie in 1902-4. Much to marvel over and wish that everybody else would go away and you could stay there for the night. There's even a library full of books to keep you occupied. Tearoom; grds. Apr-Oct 1.30-5.30pm. Helensburgh is 45km NW of city centre via Dumbarton (A82) and A814 up N Clyde coast. **ADMN**

**315**
D3 **THE WILLOW TEAROOMS:** Sauchiehall St. The café he designed (or what's left of it); certainly where to go for a tea break on the trail (155/BEST TEAROOMS).

**316**
xE3 **MARTYR'S PUBLIC SCHOOL:** 946 6600. Parson St. Latest renovation and public access to another spectacular Mackintosh building. Check those roof trusses. Phone for times. **FREE**

**317**
xA5 **HOUSE FOR AN ART LOVER:** 353 4770. Bellahouston Park. 10 Dumbreck Rd. Take the M8 W, then the M77, turn rt onto Dumbreck Rd and it's on your left. These rms were designed, nearly a century ago, specifically, it would seem, for willowy women to come and go, talking of Michelangelo. Detail is the essence of Mackintosh, and there's plenty here, but the overall effect is of space and light and a complete absence of clutter. Design shop and Exhibition Café (157/BEST TEAROOMS) on the ground floor. Daily 10am-5pm. **ADMN**

*For the current programmes of the places below and all other venues, consult The List magazine, on sale fortnightly at most newsagents.*

## CINEMA

*There are all the usual multiplexes, but the best picture houses are:*

**318**
**C3**
**GLASGOW FILM THEATRE:** 332 6535. Rose St at downtown end of Sauchiehall St. Known affectionately as GFT, has bar and 2 screens for essential art house flicks.

**319**
**A1**
**GROSVENOR:** 339 4928. Ashton Lane, off Byres Rd behind Hillhead Stn. Busy lane for eats and nightlife as well as this old cinema with 2 screens and a selected programme of mainly current hits.

## THEATRE

**320**
**D5**
✓ ✓ **THE CITIZENS:** 429 0022. Gorbals St, just over the river. Fabulous main auditorium and 2 small studios. Drama at its v best. One of Britain's most influential theatres, esp for design. Reopened after lottery-funded renovations, and taking on the world – this is the one we love!

**321**
**xC5**
✓ ✓ **THE TRAMWAY:** 422 2023. 25 Albert Dr on S side. A theatre and vast performance space. Dynamic and widely influential with an innovative and varied programme from all over the world. Seasonal programme. Re-opening at time of going to press.

**322**
**C3**
✓ **CCA:** 332 7521. Centre for Contemporary Arts, 350 Sauchiehall St. Central arts-lab complex, notable as a theatre for modern dance (esp in spring with its New Moves programme), but also has gallery and other performance space and a good café. Cl 2000 for renovation.

**323**
**D4**
✓ **THE ARCHES:** 221 9736. Midland St, betw Jamaica St and Oswald St. Experimental and vital theatre on a tight budget in the railway arches under the tracks of Central Stn. Andy Arnold will not lie down. Opening times vary. W/end clubs among the best (355/BEST CLUBS). Major millennium renovations underway at the time of going to press.

**324**
**D3**
**RSAMD:** 332 4101. 100 Renfrew St. The Royal Scottish Academy of Music and Drama. Part and wholly student productions often with guest directors. Eclectic, often powerful mix.

**325**  **THE TRON THEATRE:** 552 4267. 63 Trongate. Contemporary Scottish
*E4*  theatre and other interesting performance, esp music. Recent face-lift. Gr
café-bar with food before and *après* (85/BEST BISTROS).

**326**  **KING'S THEATRE:** 227 5511. Bath St. Trad theatre with shows like pantos,
*C3*  Gilbert and Sullivan and major touring musicals.

## CLASSICAL MUSIC

**327**  **THEATRE ROYAL:** 332 3321. Hope St. Home of Scottish Opera, with a
*D3*  mainly high-brow diet of opera, ballet (from Scottish Ballet) and some
drama.

**328**  **GLASGOW ROYAL CONCERT HALL:** 332 6633. Top of Buchanan St.
*D3*  Sep-Apr subscription series and Jun Proms from the Royal Scottish
National Orchestra, plus visits from national and international orchestras.

**329**  **CITY HALLS:** 227 5511. Candleriggs. Winter subscription series provided
*E4*  by the Scottish Chamber Orchestra and BBC Scottish Symphony
Orchestra.

**330**  **RSAMD:** 332 4101. 110 Renfrew St. Student productions often excel, plus
*D3*  recitals from high-profile international artistes.

**331**  **HUTCHESON'S HALL:** 552 8391. 158 Ingram St. Chamber concerts and
*E4*  recitals, many at lunchtime, in this NTS property.

## JAZZ

**332**  See *The List* or *Live Scene*, a monthly freesheet. Best venues: **INTERNA-
TIONAL JAZZ FESTIVAL** in early Jul (227 5511). Rest of the year: **BOUR-
BON STREET** (552 0141), **THE BABY GRAND, THE BREWERY TAP** and
**BLACKFRIARS.** Sun afternoon jazz at the **PAISLEY ARTS CENTRE,**
New St (887 1010). Occasional gigs at **PIZZA EXPRESS**, 151 Queen St
(221 3333), and concerts at the **MITCHELL THEATRE** (287 4855).

## FOLK MUSIC AND CEILIDHS

**333**  ✓ ✓ **CELTIC CONNECTIONS:** 332 6633. Major jamboree every Jan.
*D3*  3 weeks of concerts, ceilidhs and gatherings. Broad appeal.
Mainly at the Glasgow Royal Concert Hall, but also at other venues city-
wide, incl the Old Fruitmarket in Albion St.

**334** ✓ **CLUTHA VAULTS:** 167 Stockwell St. E End nr Clyde. Gr atmos for the
*D4* drink and the music. Mixed programme: readings Tue, bluegrass Sat afternoons. (204/GR GLAS PUBS)

**335** ✓ **THE HALT BAR:** Woodlands Rd. Among a mixed music programme,
*B2* always some folk for the kind of folk who inhabit the bar. (199/GR GLAS PUBS)

**336** ✓ **SCOTIA BAR:** 112 Stockwell St. The folk club and writers' retreat and
*D4* all things non-high cultural. Club meets Wed night and Sat afternoons. Always the 'right folk' here. (203/GR GLAS PUBS)

**337** ✓ **VICTORIA BAR:** Bridgegate. Nr the Scotia (*see above*) and a similar
*D4* set-up. Fri and Sat night sessions of Irish/Scottish trad music. (202/GR GLAS PUBS)

**338** ✓ **THE RENFREW FERRY:** Enter by Clyde Pl via Jamaica St Br from N
*C4* of river or Br St. A real ferry moored on the Clyde – brilliant ambience for ceilidhs and gigs of all kinds. Fri 9pm-2am. Tickets at quay or in advance from Ticket Centre, Candleriggs (227 5511), usually sold out by 10pm. Visitors and locals. Gr bands.

**339** **THE RIVERSIDE:** 248 3144. Fox St, off Clyde St. The place that started the
*D4* ceilidh revival in Glas. Upstairs in quiet st, the joint is jumping. Fri-Sat from 8pm, fills up quickly. Good bands. Good, mixed crowd.

## ROCK AND POP MUSIC

*For live music in smaller venues, see* GOOD LIVE MUSIC.

**340** ✓ ✓ ✓ **BARROWLAND BALLROOM:** Gallowgate. When its lights
*xE4* are on, you can't miss it. The Barrowland is world-famous and for many bands one of their favourite gigs. It's tacky and a bit run-down, but distinctly venerable; and with its high stage and sprung dance floor, perfect for rock 'n' roll. The Glas audience is one of 'the best in the world'. True!

**341** **SECC:** 248 3000. Finnieston Quay beyond the city centre and, for many,
*A3* beyond the pale as far as concerts are concerned (big shed, not big on atmos), but there are 3 different-sized halls for mainly arena-sized acts and everyone from Eric to Pav and Oasis have played here. Glasgow's own, Wet Wet Wet, currently hold the record for numbers of nights sold – bet we won't see that again!

**342**  **CLYDE AUDITORIUM, aka THE ARMADILLO:** Adj to the SECC. A small-
A3   er theatre space, a belter for concerts, but not big enough for the megas.

*Neither of the above venues has its own box office. For tickets and informa-*
*tion check with Tower Records, Argyle St, 204 2500 and Virgin Records,*
*Buchanan St, 353 2993 and for credit card bookings 227 5511.*

**343**  **PAVILION THEATRE:** 332 1846. Renfield St. Regular concerts and a
D3   cosier place to watch a band.

**344**
*A3* ✓ **DELMONICA'S:** 552 4803. 68 Virginia St. Refurbed stylish pub with long bar and open plan in quiet lane in Merchant City. Food till 7pm. Pally, pre-club crowd later on. Some event nights. 7 days till 12midnight.

**345**
*D4* **POLO LOUNGE:** 553 1221. 84 Wilson St. Classiest Glas gay bar yet by same people who own Delmonica's (*see above*) and Caffe Latte (*see below*). Comfortable and clubbable by day, cruisier by night. Downstairs disco (Fri-Sun) with 3am licence; otherwise till 1am (one of the few pubs in town serving after 12midnight). (245/THESE ARE HIP)

**346**
*C4* **WATERLOO BAR:** 221 7539. 306 Argyle St. Old-established bar and clientele. Not really for trendy young things. You might not fancy anybody but they're a friendly down-to-earth old bunch. 7 days till 12midnight.

**347**
*E4* **COURT BAR:** 552 2463. 69 Hutcheson St, centre of Merchant City area. Long-going small bar that's fairly straight till mid-evening. 7 days till midnight.

**348**
*D3* **SADIE FROSTS:** 332 8005. 8 W George St, in front of Queen St Stn and underneath Burger King. Downtown cruisy bar, well placed for the brief encounter. Gets jumpy nr closing time. Incorporates **SAPPHO**, a bar for pool-playing girls. 7 days till 12midnight.

**349**
*D3* **AUSTINS:** 221 0444. 61b Miller St. Glas stalwart gay bar relocated and revamped in city centre nr George Sq (Polo Lounge, etc). 7 days, bistro menu.

**350**
*D4* **BENNETS:** 552 5761. 80 Glassford St. For 20 yrs the real disco. Everybody goes in the beginning – and in the end. Late '90s face-lift, so she's looking good again. Wed-Sun 11pm-3am, Tue is 'traditionally' straight night.

## OTHER PLACES

**351**
*D4* **CAFFE LATTE:** 553 2553. Corner of Virginia St and Wilson St. Café-bistro at heart of gay st; not at all cloney. Laid-back atmos; snacks and food all day till 12midnight.

**352**
*D4* **CENTURION SAUNA:** 248 4485. 19 Dixon St, above Aer Lingus and St Enoch's. Till 10pm or later (some Sat all-nighters).

**353**
*C4* **THE LANE:** 221 1802. 60 Robertson St, nr Waterloo Bar (*see above*) opp side of Argyle St, lane on rt. You 'look for the green light'. Sauna and private club with cabins. 7 days, afternoons till 10pm.

### HOTEL

**354** **ALBION HOTEL:** 339 8620. 405 N Woodside Rd, off Gr Western Rd.
*C1* Currently Glasgow's only prospect is gay-friendly (i.e. they advertise in *Gay Times*) rather than gay. It's a start.

16RMS   JAN-DEC   T/T   XPETS   CC   KIDS   INX

*Many of the best clubs come and go and there's little point in mentioning them here. Some are only on once a week with no permanent venue. Consult The List (fortnightly) for up-to-date info, and look for flyers. Glas is a club city, but the dreaded curfew remains – check the following for current 'rules'.*

**355**
**D4**
**CLUBS AT THE ARCHES:** 221 9736. At the Arches Theatre, Midland St (322/NIGHTLIFE), w/ends only. Glasgow's finest. 2/3 vaulted archways, serious sound system and v up-for-it crowd. Major millennium makeover to building but club nights set to continue. Best clubs: Inside Out, Colours, Slam one-offs.

**356**
**D4**
**ARCHAOS:** 204 3189. 25 Queen St. Huge dance emporium on 3 floors, incl Betty's Mayonnaise. Central dance floor has state-of-the-art lighting. Balconies upstairs for action-checking and chilling. Atmos more rarified the higher you go. They'd like the Skybar to be like the Met bar.

**357**
**D4**
**YANG:** 248 8484. 31 Queen St. Same crowd as Archaos *above*, but newer and fresher. Different clubs/DJs each night but open all week from 6pm.

**358**
**C3**
**ALASKA:** 248 1777. 142 Bath Lane. Lane behind Bath St (behind the Spy Bar – 244/THESE ARE HIP – same management). Laid-back bar area, hard-hitting dance floor. Rooftop view upstairs like a New York thing.

**359**
**D4**
**THE TUNNEL:** 221 7500. 84 Mitchell St. Once defined club culture in Glas. Still high-glam quotient and designer ambience with vogue-ish crowd. W/ends (Ark and Triumph) and student nights. On same circuit as Liverpool's Cream so big-name DJs every month.

**360**
**D4**
**THE APARTMENT:** 221 7080. 23 Royal Exchange Sq. Colin and Kelly Barr's drinking club kind of disco for older, more discerning types. Exclusivity is part of the deal, but they have been known to let in any old footballer and hairdresser. Similar crowd to be found downstairs in **BABAZA** (owned by King City Leisure). Apartment open Thu–Mon from 11pm.

**361**
**C3**
**TRASH:** 572 3372. 197 Pitt St. Mega disco thing in W End. Student-ish crowd so not teensy. Clubs vary, till 3am.

**362**
**D4**
**THE SUB CLUB:** 248 4600. 22 Jamaica St. Long-running, but revamped and still v much a scene. Eclectic music policy. Fri-Sat (some Thu and Sun).

**363**
**C3**
**THE GARAGE:** 332 1120. 490 Sauchiehall St. The big night out for cheap drinks, chart sounds and copping off. Totally unpretentious. Live bands as advertised.

**BOTANIC GARDENS AND KIBBLE PALACE** 'a wonderful place to muse and wander' (page 82)

# WHERE TO GO OUT OF TOWN

# EASY WALKS OUTSIDE THE CITY

*See page 9 for walk codes. Refer to Around Glasgow map on pages 116–17.*

**364** **CAMPSIE FELLS:** Range of hills 25km N of city best reached via
**D3** Kirkintilloch or Cumbernauld/Kilsyth. Encompasses area that includes the
Kilsyth Hills, Fintry Hills and Carron Valley betw. (1) Good app from A803,
Kilsyth main st up the Tak-me-Doon (*sic*) rd. Park by the golf club and follow path by the burn. It's poss to take in the two hills to left as well as
Tomtain (453m), the most easterly of the tops, in a good afternoon; views
to the E. (2) Drive on to the jnct (9km) of the B818 rd to Fintry and go left,
following Carron Valley reservoir to the far corner where there is a
forestry rd to the left. Park here and follow track to ascend Meikle Bin
(570m) to the rt, the highest peak in the central Campsies. (3) The bonny
village of Fintry (46/HOTELS O/SIDE GLAS) is a good start/base for the Fintry
Hills and Earl's Seat (578m). (4) Campsie Glen – a sliver of glen in the hills.
App via Clachen of Campsie on A81 (decent tearoom) or from viewpoint
high on the hill on B822 from Lennoxtown to Fintry. This is the easy
Campsie intro.                                    **10KM+ CAN BE CIRC XBIKE 2-B-2**

**365** **GLENIFFER BRAES, PAISLEY:** Ridge to the S of Paisley (15km from Glas)
**D3** has been a favourite walking-place for centuries. M8 or Paisley Rd W to town
centre then: (1) S via B775/A736 towards Irvine or (2) B774
(Causewayside then Neilston Rd) and sharp rt after 3km to Glenfield Rd
(Bus: Clydeside 24). For (1) go 2km after last houses, winding up ridge and
park/start at Robertson Park (signed). Here there are superb views and
walks marked to E and W. (2) 500m along Glenfield Rd is a car park/ranger
centre. Walk up through grds and formal parkland and then W along
marked paths and trails. Eventually, after 5km, this route joins (1).
                                          **2-10KM CAN BE CIRC MTBIKE 1-A-2**

**366** **GREENOCK CUT:** 45km W of Glas. Can app via Pt Glas but simplest route
**C3** is from A78 rd to Largs. Travelling S from Greenock take first left after IBM,
signed L Thom. Lochside 5km up winding rd. Park at Cornalees Br Centre.
Walk left along lochside rd to Overton (5km) then path is signed. The Cut,
an aqueduct built in 1827 to supply water to Greenock and its 31 mills, is
now an ancient monument. Gr views from the mast over the Clyde.
Another route to the rt from Cornalees leads through a glen of birch,
rowan and oak to the Kelly Cut. Both trails described on board at the car
park.                                          **15/16KM CIRC MTBIKE 1-B-2**

**367** **MUIRSHIEL:** General name for vast area of 'Inverclyde' W of city, incl
**C3** Greenock Cut (*see above*), Castle Semple Country Park and Lunderston

Bay, a stretch of coastline nr the Cloch Lighthouse on the A770 S of Gourock for littoral amblings. But best wildish bit is Muirshiel Country Park itself, with trails, a waterfall and Windy Hill (350m). Nothing arduous, but a breath of air. From Pt Glas head S on A761 for Kilmacolm then S for Lochwinnoch on B786.

**368** **THE WHANGIE:** On A809 N from Bearsden about 8km after last r/bout
D3 and 2km after the Carbeth Inn, is the car park for the Queen's View (280/BEST VIEWS). Climb uphill towards the stand of conifers and over the stile. Of 2 paths, one leads along the top of the scarp, while the other lower down runs parallel to it and offers more protection from the elements. Both lead to the westerly end of the escarpment. Once you get to the summit of Auchineden Hill, take the path that drops down to the W (a half-rt-angle) and look for crags on your rt. This is the 'back door' of The Whangie. The path then seems to disappear into the side of the hill but carry on and you'll suddenly find yourself in a deep cleft in the rock face with sheer walls rising over 10m on either side. The Whangie is more than 100m long and at one pt the walls narrow to less than 1m. As you emerge, take the lowest path, back along the face of the hill to the stile and then down to the car park. Local mythology has it that The Whangie was made by the Devil, who lashed his tail in anticipation of a witchy rendezvous somewhere in the N, and carved a slice through the rock, where the path now goes. **5KM CIRC XBIKE XDOGS 1-A-1**

**369** **CHATELHÉRAULT, nr HAMILTON:** Jnct 6 off M74, well signposted into
D3 Hamilton, follow rd into centre, then bear left away from main rd where it's signed for A723. The gates to the 'château' are about 3km o/side town. A drive leads to the William Adam-designed hunting lodge of the Dukes of Hamilton, set amid ornamental grds with a notable parterre and extensive grounds. Tracks along the deep, wooded glen of the Avon (ruins of Cadzow Castle) lead to distant glades. Ranger service and good guided walks (01698 426213). 20km SE of city centre. Lodge open 10.30am-4.30pm, walks at all times. **2-7KM CIRC BIKE 1-A-2**

# WHERE TO TAKE KIDS

*Refer to Around Glasgow map on pages 116–17.*

**370**
**C4** ✓ **KIDZ PLAY, PRESTWICK:** 01292 475215. Off main st at Stn Rd, past stn to beach and to rt. Big shed that's a soft play area for kids. Everything that the little blighters will like in the throwing-themselves-around department. Shriek city and a non-parent nightmare zone. They never had anything like this in my day, only trees (he said, Day-Glo green with envy). 7 days, 9.30am-7pm.

**371**
**C3** **KELBURN COUNTRY CENTRE, LARGS:** 2km S of Largs on A78. Riding school, grds, woodland walks up the Kel Burn and a central visitor/consumer section with shops/exhibs/cafés. Wooden stockade for clambering kids; commando assault course for exhibitionist adults and less doddering dads. Falconry displays (and long-suffering owl). Kelburn continues to develop its range of attractions: a Secret Forest has appeared in the woods. Combine with Vikingar! (*see below*) for an exhausting day. Stock up with chips and Nardini's ice cream (411/O/SIDE GLAS). 7 days, 10am-6pm.

**372**
**D4** **LOUDON CASTLE, nr GALSTON:** Theme park in S of Glas hinterland. Just off A71 Kilmarnock–Edin rd (go from Glas via A77 Kilmarnock rd). Behind the ruins of the said Loudon Castle (burned out in 1941) a fairground incl the 'largest carousel in Europe' and massive 'chairy-plane' has been transplanted in the old walled grd. Nice setting: well, kids might not notice the setting, but they won't forget the chairy-plane. Open AYR, 10am-dusk.

**373**
**E3** **PALACERIGG COUNTRY PARK, CUMBERNAULD:** 01236 720047. 6km E of Cumbernauld. 740 acres of parkland; ranger service, nature trails, picnic area and kids' farm. 18-hole golf course and putting green. Exhib area with changing exhibs about forestry, conservation, etc. Open AYR daylight hrs. Visitor centre and tearoom until 6.30pm summer, 4.30pm winter.

**374**
**E3** **THE TIME CAPSULE, MONKLANDS:** 01236 449572. They say Monklands, but where you are going is downtown Coatbridge, about 15km from Glas via the M8. Known rather meanly as the 'Tim Capture' (local joke – you don't want to know!). Essentially a leisure (rather than a swimming) pool and ice rink lavishly fitted out on prehistoric monster theme. Even if you haven't been swimming for yrs, this is the sort of place you force the flab into the swimsuit. Cafés and view areas. Facs of the clean-up-your-act variety (e.g. squash, sauna, sun, steam, gym). 'Courses.' 10am-10pm.

**375** **VIKINGAR!, LARGS:** Suddenly fulfilled all the needs and gaps in this
*C3* busy visitor area of the Clyde coast – a pool and sports centre, a theatre,
an indoor attraction and a dab of heritage. Got the award. But hey . . . it
works. It won't exercise your intellect, but the other bits will do just fine. 7
days, 10.30am-6pm (till 4pm in winter).

**376** **DOLLAN AQUA CENTRE, TOWN CENTRE PARK, EAST KILBRIDE:**
*D3* 01355 260000. EK: The 'Gr Experiment' in New Town planning boasts a
quality leisure centre. 50m pool, fitness facs, soft play area and Scotland's
first interactive flume (aquatic pinball machine with you as the ball –
there had to be a twist!). Mon-Wed 7.30am-10pm, Thu-Fri 8am-10pm, Sat-
Sun 8am-6pm. Last sessions 2 hrs before closing.

# THE BEST PLACES OUTSIDE GLASGOW

*Refer to Around Glasgow map on pages 116–17.*

## HISTORICAL PLACES

**377**
*C4*
✔✔ **CULZEAN CASTLE, MAYBOLE:** 24km S of Ayr on A719. Impossible to convey here the scale and the scope of the house and country park. Allow some hrs esp for the grounds. Castle is more like a country house and you examine from other side of a rope. From the 12th century but rebuilt by Robert Adam in 1775, a time of soaring ambition, its grandeur is almost out of place in this exposed clifftop position. It was designed for entertaining and the oval staircase is magnificent. Wartime associations (esp with President Eisenhower, which will interest Americans), plus the enduring fascination of the aristocracy. 560 acres of grounds, incl clifftop walk, formal grds, walled grd, Swan Pond (a must) and Happy Valley. Harmonious home farm is a visitor centre with café, exhibs, shop, etc. Apr-Oct 10am-5pm. Culzean is pronounced 'Cullane'.

**378**
*D3*
✔✔ **PAISLEY ABBEY:** Town centre. An abbey founded in 1163, razed by the English in 1307 and with successive deteriorations and renovations ever since. Major restoration in the 1920s brought it to present-day cathedral-like magnificence. Exceptional stained glass (the recent window complementing the formidable Strachan E Window), an impressive choir and an edifying sense of space. Sun services (11am and 6.30pm) are superb, esp full-dress communion, and there are open days (about one Sat a month, phone TO 889 0711) with coffee in the cloisters, organ music and the tower open for climbing. Otherwise abbey open AYR 10am-3.30pm. Café/shop. (284/BEST VIEWS)

**379**
*D3*
**BOTHWELL CASTLE, UDDINGSTON:** 15km E of Glas via M74, Uddingston t/off into main st and follow signs. Hugely impressive 13th-century ruin, the home of the Black Douglases, o/looking the Clyde. Remarkable considering proximity to city that there is hardly any 20th-century intrusion except yourself. Pay to go inside. Walk down to Clyde and enjoy riverside trails to Blantyre.

**380**
*D3*
**HAMILTON MAUSOLEUM, STRATHCLYDE PARK:** Off (and visible from) M74 at jnct 5/6, 15km from Glas. Huge over-the-top/over-the-tomb (though removed 1921) stone memorial to the 10th Duke of Hamilton. Guided tours daily (Easter-Sep at 3pm and, even better, evenings in Jul

and Aug at 7pm; winter Sat-Sun at 3pm). Eerie and chilling and with remarkable acoustics – the 'longest echo in Europe'. Give it a shout or take your violin.

**381** **CROSSRAGUEL ABBEY, MAYBOLE:** 24km S of Ayr on A77. Built 1244,
*C4* one of the first Cluniac settlements in Scotland, an influential and rich order, stripped in the Reformation. Now an extensive ruin of architectural distinction, the ground plan is v well preserved and obvious. Open daily.

**CHATELHÉRAULT, nr HAMILTON:** Report: 369/WALKS O/SIDE THE CITY.

## OUTDOOR PLACES

**382** ✓ ✓ **THE YOUNGER BOTANIC GARDEN, BENMORE:** 12km from
*C3* Dunoon on the A815 to Strachur. An 'outstation' of the Royal Botanic in Edin, gifted to the nation by Harry the Younger in 1928, but the first plantations dating from 1820. Walks clearly marked through formal grds, woody grounds and the 'pinetum' where the air is so sweet and spicy it can seem like the v elixir of life. Redwood ave, terr hillsides, views; a grd of different moods and fine proportions. Café. Apr-Oct 10am-6pm.
**ADMN**

**383** ✓ ✓ **ROTHESAY–TIGNABRUAICH:** A886/A8003. The most cele-
*C3* brated part of this route is the latter, the A8003 down the side of L Riddon to Tignabruaich along the hillsides which give the breathtaking views of Bute and the Kyles, but the whole way, with its diverse aspects of lochside, riverine and rocky scenery, is supernatural. Incl short ferry crossing between Rhubodach and Colintraive.

**384** ✓ **OSTAL BEACH/KILBRIDE BAY, MILLHOUSE, nr TIGNABRU-**
*C3* **AICH:** Down rd from 'Millhouse corner' on B8000, a track to the rt at a white house (there's a church on the left) marked 'Private road, no cars' (often with a chain across to restrict access). Park and walk 1km, turning rt after lochan. You arrive on a perfect white sandy crescent known locally as Ostal and, apart from stranded jellyfish and the odd swatch of sewage, in certain conditions, a mystical secret place to swim and picnic. The N coast of Arran is like a Greek island in the bay.

**385** **FALLS OF CLYDE, NEW LANARK:** Dramatic falls in a long gorge of the
*E3* Clyde. New Lanark, the conservation village of Robert Owen the social reformer, is signed from Lanark. It's hard to avoid the 'award-winning'

tourist bazaar, but I'd recommend getting out of the village and along the riverbank ASAP. The path to the power stn is about 3km, but the route doesn't get interesting until after it, a 1km climb to the first fall (Cora Linn) and another 1km to the next (Bonnington Linn). Swimming above or below them is not advised (but it's gr). Certainly don't swim on an 'open day', when they close the stn and divert all the water back down the river in a mighty surge (about once a month in summer on Sun, phone TO 01555 661661).

**386** **STRATHCLYDE PARK, betw HAMILTON and MOTHERWELL:** 15km
**E3** SE of Glas. Take M8/A725 interchange or M74 jnct 5 or 6. Scotland's most popular country park, esp for watersports on the 'man-made' lake. Everything from canoeing to parascending and you can hire all the gear there. Also excavated Roman bath house, playgrounds, sports pitches and now that the trees are beginning to mature, some pleasant walks too. Also Hamilton Mausoleum (*see above*). Nearby Baron's Haugh and Dalzell Country Park more notable for their nature trails and grds. (31/CAMPING)

**387** **LOCHWINNOCH:** 30km SW of Glas via M8 jnct 29 then A737 and A760
**C3** past Johnstone. Also from Largs 20km via A760. A nature reserve just o/side the village on lochside and comprising wetland and woodland habitats. A serious 'nature centre' incorporating an observation tower. Hides and marked trails; and a birds-spotted board. Shop and coffee shop. Good for kids. Centre 10am-5pm. (33/CAMPING)

**388** **EGLINTON COUNTRY PARK, nr IRVINE:** Beside main A78 Largs–Ayr
**C4** rd signed from Irvine/Kilwinning intersection. Spacious lungful of Ayrshire nr new town nexus and traffic tribulations. Visitor centre with interpretation of absolutely everything; network of walks. Not much left of the house. A factory makes 'ambient foods'. All a bit of a construct, but some parts are peaceful.

## HILLS

**389** **CONIC HILL, BALMAHA, LOCH LOMOND:** An easier climb than the
**D2** Ben up the rd (*see below*) and a good place to view it from, Conic, on the Highland fault line, is one of the first Highland hills you reach from Glas. Stunning views also of L Lomond from its 358m peak. Ascend through woodland from the corner of Balmaha car park. Watch for buzzards and your footing on the final crumbly bits. 1.5 hrs up. **2-A-2**

**390** **BEN LOMOND, ROWARDENNAN, LOCH LOMOND:** Many folk's first
*D2* Munro, given proximity to Glas (soul and city). It's not too taxing a climb
Munro-wise and has rewarding views (in good weather). 2 main ascents:
'tourist route' is easier, from toilet block at Rowardennan car park (end of
rd from Drymen), well trodden all the way; or 500m up past youth hostel,
a path follows burn – the 'Ptarmigan route'. Circular walk possible. 3 hrs
up.                                                                                                        **2-A-2**

**391** **TINTO HILL, betw BIGGAR and LANARK:** A favourite climb in
*E4* S/Central Scotland with easy access to start from A73 nr Symington,
10km S of Lanark. Park 100m behind Tinto Hills farm shop, after stocking
up with rolls and juice. Good track, though it has its ups and downs before
you get there. Braw views. 707m. Allow 3 hrs.                                         **2-A-2**

**392** **THE COBBLER (BEN ARTHUR), ARROCHAR:** Perennial favourite of
*C2* the Glas hill walker and, for sheer exhilaration, the most popular of 'the
Arrochar Alps'. A motorway path ascends from the A83 on the other side
of L Long from Arrochar (park in the new car park at the head of the loch)
and it takes 2.5-3 hrs to traverse the up 'n' down route to the top. Just
short of a Munro at 881m, it has 3 tops, of which the N peak is the simplest scramble (central and S peaks for climbers). Way isn't marked; con-
sult map or other walkers.                                                              **2-B-3**

## GOLF

**393** **✓ TURNBERRY:** 01655 331000. Ailsa (championship) and Arran.
*C4* Sometimes poss by application. Otherwise you must stay at the
hotel. Superb.

**394** **✓ ROYAL OLD COURSE, TROON:** V difficult to get on. No wimmen.
*C4* Staying at Marine Highland Hotel (01292 314444) helps. Easier is
**THE PORTLAND COURSE**: across rd from Royal. Both 01292 311555.

**395** **GLASGOW GAILES/WESTERN GAILES:** 01294 311347/311649.
*C4* Superb links courses next to one another, 5km S of Irvine off the A78.

**396** **OLD PRESTWICK:** 01292 477404. Original home of the Open and 'every
*C4* challenge you'd wish to meet'. Hotels opp (e.g. the Golf View, 01292
671234) cost less than a round. Unlikely to get on at w/ends.

**397** **BELLEISLE, AYR:** 01292 441258. Good parkland course. Easy to get on.
*C4*

**398** **ROTHESAY:** 01700 503554. Sloping golf course with breathtaking views
C3   of Clyde. Visitors welcome. What could be finer than taking the train from
Glas to Wemyss Bay for the ferry over and 18 holes. Finish up with fish 'n'
chips at The W End on the way home.

**399** **LOCH LOMOND GOLF COURSE, LUSS:** On A82 1km from conserva-
D2   tion village of Luss. Exclusive American-owned club; membership only
5000 bucks! We can buy a cheaper season ticket to see the annual World
Invitational tournament (early Jul; tickets 0990 661661); but no access to
plebs to clubhouse. 18 holes of scenic golf by the loch. This is golfing for
gold.

## WATER SPORTS

**400** **KIP MARINA, INVERKIP:** 01475 521485. Major sailing centre on Clyde
C3   coast 50km W of Glas via M8, A8 and A78 from Pt Glas heading S for Largs.
A yacht heaven as well as haven of Grand Prix status. Sails, charters,
pub/restau, chandlers and myriad boats. Diving equipment, jet skis and
dinghies for hire.

**401** ✓ **GOUROCK BATHING POOL:** 01475 315611. One of only 2 remain-
C3   ing (proper) open-air pools in Scotland that are still open. On coast
rd S of town centre 45km from central Glas. 1950s- style leisure. Heated,
so it doesn't need to be a scorcher (brilliant, but crowded when it is).
Open 'in season' 10am-8pm, Sun till 5pm.

**402** ✓ **STRATHCLYDE PARK WATERSPORTS:** 01698 266155. Major
E3   watersports centre 15km SE of Glas and easily reached from most of
Central Scotland via M8 or M74 (jnct 5 or 6). 200 acre loch and centre with
instruction on sailing, canoeing, windsurfing, rowing and waterskiing, and
hire facs for canoes, Mirrors and Wayfarers, windsurfers and trimarans.
Sessions: summer 9.30am-10pm; winter 9.30am-5pm. (33/CAMPING)

**403** **CASTLE SEMPLE COUNTRY PARK, LOCHWINNOCH:** 01505 842882.
C3   30km SW of Glas off M8 at jnct 29, A737 then A760 past Johnstone. Also
25km from Largs via A760. Loch nr village is 3km by 1km and at the
Rangers Centre you can hire windsurfers, dinghies, canoes, etc. Bird
reserve on opp bank. Peaceful place to learn.

**TIME CAPSULE, MONKLANDS:** Report: 374/WHERE TO TAKE KIDS.

## WHERE TO EAT OUTSIDE GLASGOW

**404**
**D2**
✔ **THE BLACK BULL HOTEL, KILLEARN:** 01360 550215. 2 The Sq. Good-looking village, 30 min N of Glas betw L Lomond (Drymen) and the Campsies. Excellent pub food and conservatory restau. Good service (owners had hotel in US); waiters have ear pieces! Imaginative cuisine way beyond usual pub standard. Excellent puds. Live jazz. (38/HOTELS O/SIDE TOWN, 141/KID-FRIENDLY) **MED**

**405**
**C3**
✔ **BRAIDWOODS, nr DALRY:** 01294 833544. Off main A78 coast rd, take Dalry rd at Saltcoats, 6km along country rd: the Braidwoods' whitewashed cottages and Keith's legendary cooking. This is better than most of Glas and much better value (incl wines). Wed/Sat lunch and dinner, and Sun lunch. **MED**

**406**
**E3**
✔ **RISTORANTE LA VIGNA, LANARK:** 01555 664320. 40 Wellgate. Famously good Italian restau in a back st in Lanark. 7 days, lunch and dinner. Must book. **MED**

**407**
**C3**
✔ **FINS, FAIRLIE, nr LARGS:** 01475 568989. On main A78 8km S of Largs, a seafood bistro, smokery, shop and craft/cookshop. This place is altogether good. Chef Gillian Dick uses exemplary restraint and the wine list is similarly to the point. Lunch and dinner. Cl Mon. **INX**

**408**
**D2**
✔ **THE CROSS KEYS, KIPPEN:** 01786 870293. An inn that's been here forever in this quiet backwater town off the A811 15km W of Stirling. Bar meals by coal fire, à la carte and family restaus. A real pub food haven, and about the only thing Egon Ronay has got right around here. LO 8.45pm.

**409**
**C4**
✔ **WHEATSHEAF INN, SYMINGTON, nr AYR:** 01563 830307. 2km off the A77. Pleasant village off the unpleasant A77 with this busy coaching inn opp church. Folk come from miles around to eat (book at w/ends) honest-to-goodness pub fare in various rms (roast beef every Sun). Menu on boards. LO 10pm.

**410**
**D2**
**LA SCARPETTA, BALLOCH:** 01389 758247. Balloch Rd. Not perhaps many reasons to linger in Balloch (the loch here is not one of them), but if on a sojourn to L Lomond or points NW, this is an excellent Italian restau. Favourite of writer A.L. Kennedy, and she ain't easy to please. 7 days, LO 10pm. **MED**

**FOX AND HOUNDS, HOUSTON:** Report: 239/PUB FOOD.

## OTHER MUSTS

**411**
**C3**
✓ ✓ ✓ **NARDINI'S, LARGS:** 01475 674555. The Esplanade, Glas side. An institution. The epitome of the seaside cafeteria and all the nostalgia of Doon the Watter days. This airy brasserie with cake, ice cream and chocolate counters and in the back a trad tratt with full Italian à la carte and OK wines has a timeless formula which works today as well as it ever did. The light fittings, like almost everything else, are true originals. Summer evenings with the long light and a bowl of ice cream and the place busy with all kinds of folk is life-affirming stuff. Get you down there. High tea (4-6pm) is always a good idea. Summer till 10.30pm, winter till 8pm.

**412**
**D3**
**TORTOLANO'S, UDDINGSTON:** 29 Main St. 15km E of Glas via M74, Uddingston t/off, at the lights where you turn for Bothwell Castle (*see above*). Tiny confectioners/ice-cream shop with proper biscuit cones as an option and 5 flavours (try their 'double cream') all home-made by Montecassino's Mr Tortolano. Their loss, definitely our weight gain.

**413**
**D3**
**COLPI'S, MILNGAVIE:** Opp Black Bull in Milngavie (pronounced 'Mullguy') centre and there since 1928. Many consider this to be Glasgow's finest. Only vanilla at the cone counter but strawberry/chocolate flake/amaretto/honeycomb to take home. There's another branch in Clydebank. 7 days, till 9pm.

**414**
**D3**
✓ ✓ **FINDLAY CLARK, MILNGAVIE:** In Campsie country N of city, 20km from centre via A81 and A807 (Milngavie or Kirkintilloch rds) or heading for Milngavie, turn rt on Boclair Rd. Vast grd complex and all-round visitor experience – an institution. 'Famous' coffee shop (the famous waitresses tend to be local babes, but by no means all of them), saddlery with everything except horses; labels from Crabtree and Evelyn to Fisons, plus books, clothes and piles of plants; and live pets. 9am-8pm (till 6pm in winter).

**415**
**E3**
**CARFIN GROTTO, MOTHERWELL:** A723 just o/side Motherwell 4km from M8, on left after 2nd garage. A homage to Lourdes, built largely by striking miners in 1921. (God's) acre of grds and pathways with reliquaries, shrines, a glass pavilion and chapel. The ghost of Ravenscraig is always in the background. Spiritual sustenance, despite the throngs, for the true believers; something of a curiosity for the rest of us. Pilgrimage centre and tearoom. Open at all times.

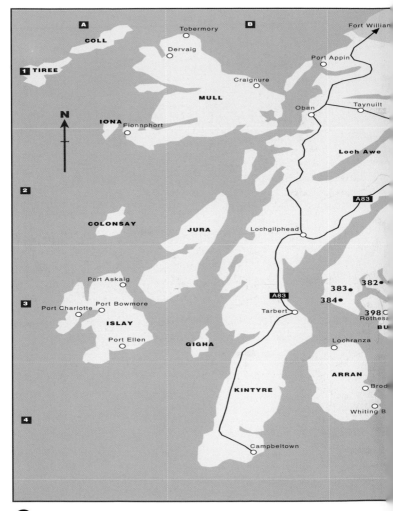

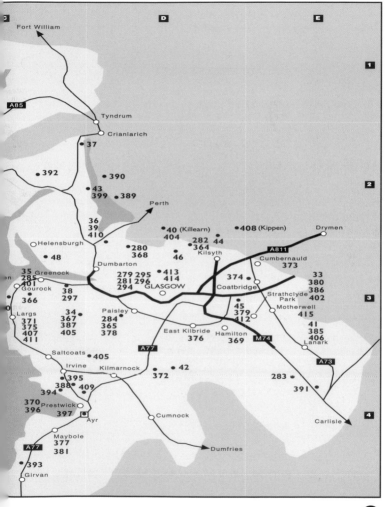

**C**

Fort William

A85

Tyndrum

Crianlarich

●37

●392

●390

●43
399  ●389

36
39
410

●40 (Killearn)     ●408 (Kippen)     Drymen

●D

●E

**1**

**2**

Perth

404           282 44
              364

○Helensburgh        ●280     46        Kilsyth
                    368

●48

Dumbarton

A811

Cumbernauld
373

35 Greenock     279 295    ●413
285              281 296    414        374
401             294
Gourock  ●38        ○GLASGOW      Coatbridge
366      297

33
380
386
Strathclyde  402
Park
Motherwell
415

**3**

Largs    34      Paisley○        45
371      367              284     379
375      387            365      412
407      405            378
411

East Kilbride       Hamilton
                376   369    M74

41
385
406
Lanark

Saltcoats ●405

A77

283 ●

391 ●

A73

Irvine
395
388 ●409
394

Kilmarnock  ●42
372

370
396  Prestwick
397    Ayr

Cumnock

Carlisle

**4**

Maybole
377
381

Dumfries

●393
Girvan

# THE VERY BEST SHOPS

*These are the shops that get it right. Glaswegians in the know go here.*

## FOOD AND DRINK

**BAKERS**

General     **BRADFORD'S**, 245 Sauchiehall St. 332 2057.
Also other branches around town.

Bread     **BAKEHAUS**, 387 Gr Western Rd. 334 5501.

Pâtisserie     **PATISSERIE FRANÇOISE**, 138 Byres Rd. 334 1351.

**BUTCHERS**     **GILLESPIE'S**, 1601 Gr Western Rd, Anniesland. 959 2015.
**JAMES ALLEN**, 85 Lauderdale Grds. 334 8973.
**MURRAY'S**, 121 Royston Rd. 552 2201.

**DELICATESSEN**

General     **FRATELLI SARTI**, 133 Wellington St. 248 2228.
**PECKHAM'S**, 100 Byres Rd. Also at Central Stn, Clarence Dr and Glassford St.
**COOKERY BOOK**, 20 Kilmarnock Rd. 632 9807.
**TOSCANA**, 44 Station Rd, Milngavie. 956 4020.
**LA TEA DOH**, 126 Nithsdale Rd, Pollokshields. 424 3224.

Cheese     **I.J. MELLIS**, 492 Gr Western Rd. 339 8998.

**FISHMONGERS**     **ALAN BEVERIDGE**, 188 Byres Rd. 357 2766. Also at 7 Station Rd, Milngavie. 956 1679.
**FISH PLAICE**, alley of Saltmarket by St Andrews St. 552 2337.
**MACCALLUM'S**, 944 Argyle St. 334 5680. Also at 455 Gr Western Rd.

**FISH 'N' CHIPS**     **UNIQUE**, 223 Allison St. 423 3366.
**PHILADELPHIA**, 445 Gt Western Rd. 339 2372.
**UNIVERSITY CAFÉ**, 83 Byres Rd. 334 9813.

**FRUIT AND VEG**     **ROOTS AND FRUITS**, 457 Gt Western Rd. 339 5164. Also at 355 Byres Rd. 334 3530.

**NO. 1 FOR VALUE**, 61 Candleriggs, by the City Hall.

**ICE CREAM**
**COLPI**, Milngavie Centre, Newton Mearns and Clydebank.
**QUEEN'S CAFÉ**, 515 Victoria Rd. 423 2409.
**UNIVERSITY CAFÉ**, 87 Byres Rd. 334 9813.
**CAFÉ AMALFI**, 55 Mt Annan Dr, King's Park. 632 2814.

**LATE-NIGHT**
**ALLDAYS**, 24 hr general store at Kelvinbridge
**GOODIE'S**, 24 hr general store at 645 Gr Western Rd. 334 8848.
**FRIENDLY'S**, 24 hr general stores at Elmbank St and Sauchiehall St.

**PASTA**
**FAZZI BROTHERS**, 67 Cambridge St. 332 0941.
**FRATELLI SARTI**, 133 Wellington St. 248 2228.

**WHOLEFOODS**
**GRASSROOTS**, 48 Woodlands Rd. 353 3278.
**QUALITY DELI**, 123 Douglas St. 331 2984.

**WINE AND BEER**
**UBIQUITOUS CHIP WINES**, 12 Ashton Lane. 334 5007.
**FRATELLI SARTI**, 121 Bath St. Also at Wellington St – *see* Pasta.
**PECKHAM AND RYE**, 21 Clarence Dr. 334 4312.
**LITTLE ITALY**, 205 Byres Rd. 339 6287.

## HOUSE AND HOME

**CERAMICS**
**NANCY SMILLIE**, Princes Sq. 248 3874.

**DEPARTMENT STORES**
**FRASERS**, 45 Buchanan St. 221 3880.
**JOHN LEWIS**, Buchanan Galleries. 353 6677.
**DEBENHAMS**, 97 Argyle St. 221 9820.

**FLOWERS**
**General**
**ROOTS AND FRUITS AND FLOWERS**, 451 Gr Western Rd. 334 5817.
**Dried**
**INSCAPE**, 141 Gr Western Rd. 332 6125.

# The Very Best Shops

**FURNITURE**
   **Modern**      **INHOUSE**, 26 Wilson St. 552 5902.
   **Traditional**  **ADRIENNE'S**, 28 Park Rd. 334 5943.
   **Interiors**    **INHOUSE**, 26 Wilson St. 552 5902.
                  **DESIGNWORKS**, 38 Gibson St. 339 9520.
                  **HABITAT**, Buchanan Galleries. 331 2233.

**IRONMONGERS**   **CROCKETS**, 136 W Nile St. 332 1041.

## CLOTHES AND APPEARANCE

**BARBERS**        **CITY BARBERS**, 99 W Nile St. 332 7114.
                  **SALANDINI'S**, 342 W Princes St. 334 1064.

**CHILDREN'S**   **STRAWBERRY FIELDS**, 517 Gr Western Rd. 339 1121.
**CLOTHES**      **PETITE VIP**, 41 Stockwell St. 552 5266.

**HAIRDRESSERS**   **RITA RUSK**, 49 W Nile St. 221 1472.
                  **DLC**, Mitchell Lane. 204 2020.
                  **LISA CASSIDY**, 18 Wilson St. 552 9904.
                  **KAVANAGH HAIRDRESSING**, 65 Virginia St. 552 8651.
                  **PELE HAIRDRESSING**, 63 Bath St. 332 7771.

**HATS**          **PANDORA'S HATS**, 5 Sinclair Dr, Battlefield. 649 7714.

**JEWELLERY**     **ARGYLE ARCADE**, Argyle St to Buchanan St. A vast array of
                  different jewellers.
                  **SHEILA MILLER DESIGNER JEWELLERY**, Princes Sq. 221
                  1248.

**LINGERIE**      **SILKS**, 675 Clarkston Rd. 633 0442.
                  **PAMOAS LINGERIE**, 78 Hyndland St. 357 2383.
                  **LA SENZA**, Buchanan Galleries. 353 6515.
                  **HEAVEN OR HELL**, 54 Wilson St. 552 9977.

## MEN'S CLOTHES

**New Labels**
**CRUISE**, 180 Ingram St. 229 0000.
**SLATER MENSWEAR**, 165 Howard St. 552 7171.
**ITALIAN CENTRE**, John St. Shops dedicated to Versace, Armani, etc.
**REISS**, Princes Sq, Buchanan St. 204 1449.
**JIGSAW**, 32 Royal Exchange Sq. 221 5942. Also at 59 Buchanan St. 248 9004.

**Old Clothes**
**BOEM SCIFRA**, De Courcey's Arcade, Cresswell Lane. 357 1335.
**FLIP**, 72 Queen St. 221 2041.
**THE SQUARE YARD**, Stevenson St W at The Barras.
**RETRO**, 8 Otago St. 576 0165.

**Outdoor Clothes**
**GRAHAM TISO**, 129 Buchanan St. 248 4877.
**BLACK'S**, 254 Sauchiehall St. 353 2344.
**NATURE BOUND**, 34 Gibson St. 337 6737.

## SHOES

**Shoes that Last**
**ROBERT JENKINS**, 183 Hyndland Rd. 334 8547. Also at 14 Royal Exchange Sq. 248 3743.

**Modish**
**SCHUH**, 45 Union St. 221 1093.
**ASPECTO**, 20 Gordon St. 248 2532.

## SPORTS

**NEVIS SPORT**, 261 Sauchiehall St. 332 4814.
**BOARDWISE**, 1146 Argyle St. 334 5559.

## WOMEN'S CLOTHES

**Established Labels**
**FRASERS**, 45 Buchanan St. 221 3880.

**Hip**
**MELLO**, Virginia St. 552 5656.
**CONCRETE SKATES**, 20 Wilson St. 552 0222.
**TRIBAL JUNKI,** 67-69 Candleriggs. 552 7078. Also at Flip basement, 72 Queen St. 221 2975.

**New Labels**
**CRUISE**, 180 Ingram St. 229 0000.
**MAXXI**, 162 Fenwick Rd. 620 3133.
**MOON**, 10 Ruthven Lane. 339 2315.

**ITALIAN CENTRE**, John St. Shops dedicated to Versace, Armani, Mondi, etc.
**HILLARY ROHDE**, 332 4147 (exclusive cashmere by appointment only).

## MISCELLANEOUS

**ANTIQUES**
**General**       **HERITAGE HOUSE**, Unit 39, Yorkhill Quay. 550 8770.
                  **RETRO**, 8 Otago St. 576 0165.
**Bric-a-brac**   **ALL OUR YESTERDAYS**, 6 Park Rd. 334 7788.
**Clothes**       **STARRY STARRY NIGHT**, 19 Dowanside Lane. 337 1837.
**Jewellery**     **VICTORIAN VILLAGE AND SARATOGA TRUNK**, 57 W Regent St. 332 0808.

**ART SUPPLIES**  **MILLERS**, Stockwell St. 553 1660. Also at Dalhousie St. 331 1661.
                  **ART STORE**, 94 Queen St. 221 0266.

**CARDS**         **PAPYRUS**, 374 Byres Rd. 334 6514. Also at 296 Sauchiehall St. 353 2182.
                  **PHOENIX GRAPHICS**, 254 Sauchiehall St. 353 0102.
                  **ILLUMINATI**, Princes Sq, Buchanan St. 204 2361.
                  **PAPERCHASE** in **BORDERS**, 98 Buchanan St. 222 7700.

**CHILDREN'S**    **THE SENTRY BOX**, 175 Gr George St. 334 6070.
**TOYS**          **THE BIG TOP**, 45 King St. 552 7763.

**COLLECTABLES**  **RELICS**, Dowanside Lane. 341 0007.
                  **JADES**, 1121 Maryhill Rd. 946 2920.
                  **KOLLECTABLES**, 51 Parnie St. 552 2208.

**COMICS**        **FUTURESHOCK**, 88 Byres Rd. 339 8184.
                  **FORBIDDEN PLANET**, 168 Buchanan St. 331 1215.
                  **A1 COMICS**, 31-35 Parnie St. 552 6692.

**GAMES**
  General      **GAMES WORKSHOP**, 66 Queen St. 226 3762.
  PC/Console  **C.A. GAMES**, De Courcey's Arcade, Cresswell Lane. 334 3901.
  **G FORCE**, 77 Union St. 248 8272.

**JOKES**             **TAM SHEPHERD'S**, 33 Queen St. 221 2310.
  **THE PARTY SHOP**, 201 Sauchiehall St. 332 3392.

**JUNK**               **THE BARRAS** (*see* **Other Attractions**)

**LATE CHEMISTS**  **MUNRO'S**, 693 Gr Western Rd. 339 0012.
  **C. & M. MACKIE**, 1067 Pollokshaws Rd. 649 8915.

**NEWSPAPERS**  **NEWSPAPER KIOSK**, Buchanan St opposite Buchanan Galleries Shopping Centre.
  **BARRETTS**, 263 Byres Rd. 339 0488.
  **JOHN SMITH**, 57 St Vincent St. 221 7472.

**PRESENTS**      **EVOLUTION**, 396 Byres Rd. 334 3200.
  **NICE HOUSE**, Italian Centre, John St. 553 1377.
  **PAST TIMES**, 70 Buchanan St. 226 2277.
  **INHOUSE**, 24 Wilson St. 552 5902.

**TOBACCO**      **ROBERT GRAHAM & CO.**, 71 St Vincent St. 221 6588.
  **TOBACCO HOUSE**, 9 St Vincent Pl. 226 4586.

**SOUVENIRS**
  Tartan/Serious  **HECTOR RUSSELL**, 10 Buchanan St. 221 0217.
  **GEOFFREY'S**, 309 Sauchiehall St. 331 2388.
  Tartan/Tacky  **DROOKO**, 11 St Vincent St. 221 7408.

# INDEX

# Other Collins Scottish Titles

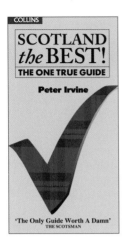

**Scotland the Best!**
(ISBN 0 00 472399-6, priced £12.99)

**Edinburgh the Best!**
(ISBN 0 00 472464-X, priced £6.99)

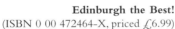

**Edinburgh Step by Step**
(ISBN 0 00 472346-5, priced £6.99)